LITERATURE AND LIBERALISM
WITH OTHER CLASSICAL PAPERS

LITERATURE
AND
LIBERALISM
WITH OTHER CLASSICAL PAPERS

BY

NELSON GLENN McCREA

ANTHON PROFESSOR OF THE LATIN
LANGUAGE AND LITERATURE

WITH A FOREWORD BY
NICHOLAS MURRAY BUTLER

1754 1893
COLUMBIA
UNIVERSITY
PRESS
IN·LITTERIS·LIBERTAS

NEW YORK: MORNINGSIDE HEIGHTS
COLUMBIA UNIVERSITY PRESS
1936

FOREIGN AGENTS

OXFORD UNIVERSITY PRESS
HUMPHREY MILFORD, AMEN HOUSE
LONDON, E.C.4, ENGLAND

KWANG HSUEH PUBLISHING HOUSE
140 PEKING ROAD
SHANGHAI, CHINA

MARUZEN COMPANY, LTD.
6 NIHONBASHI, TORI-NICHOME
TOKYO, JAPAN

OXFORD UNIVERSITY PRESS
B. I. BUILDING, NICOL ROAD
BOMBAY, INDIA

PRINTED IN THE UNITED STATES OF AMERICA

IN LVMINE TVO
VIDEBIMVS LVMEN[1]

Huc ades, Lux increata,
gentibus desiderata,
Lux vitae signifera;
Almam Matrem tu sustentes,
in tenebris quae sedentes
erigat lucifera.

Haec tuo subter vexillo
impleat vultu tranquillo
munera scientiae;
pax florescat, fraus marcescat,
Hac docente semper crescat
robur innocentiae.

Huius nos amore vincti,
ampliore spe instincti,
consulamus patriae;
ius tuentem confirmemus,
fas verentem consecremus
carae vi Columbiae.

Sic vigescet veri testis
Civitas Dei terrestris
sancto plena numine;
sic laborum nos securos
lumen diriges visuros
in tuopte lumine.

[1] Written for the *Columbia University Hymnal* (The H. W. Gray Co., 1921).
First published in *The Columbia University Quarterly,* March, 1916.

FOREWORD

THE MOST GRIEVOUS happening in the intellectual life
of the present generation is the passing of the knowledge of the classical literature and philosophy of ancient
Greece and Rome, as well as of any intelligent interest in
these. For a thousand years the literature, the philosophy
and the law of those great peoples shaped the course of a
steadily rising, deepening and broadening civilization
and offered it standards of judgment and of taste, as well
as ideals, which must always command the admiration
and the enthusiasm of the true scholar. No amount of
concern with what are called contemporary problems
can possibly take the place of a study of the origin of
those problems, of their evolution, of their many-sided
nature and of their past history.

It remains one of the wonders of the world that ancient
Greece and ancient Rome, with their very limited knowledge of nature and its forces, should have reached such
stupendous heights of accomplishment in all that relates
to the mind and to its expression in literature, in art, in
law and in institutional life. If all knowledge of classical
literature and history is to pass from the education of
today and tomorrow, then our intellectual life is to receive a blow from which it will not recover for generations — perhaps for centuries. Excellence knows no rival,
and excellence was the mark of the great achievements of
the intellectual life of those who made Athens and Rome
the leaders of the world's thought and action.

Professor Nelson Glenn McCrea has been a lifelong
student and teacher in this great field of knowledge and

has proved himself a scholar of the finest and the highest type. He has seen into and beneath the languages of those ancient peoples and has used knowledge of those languages as the open door to an understanding and an ability to interpret the thought that lies beyond which it would not be easy to equal. He has absorbed classical knowledge into his very nature, and it has long characterized and shaped not only his teaching but his personal thought and all expression of it. The papers which this volume contains reveal Professor McCrea's understanding and power in convincing fashion. Every reader of these pages will realize that he is hearing the voice of a master interpreter of ancient Greece and Rome in terms of the intellectual and moral needs of today and tomorrow. The notion that the classics are out of date because they are old is a form of silliness which it is difficult to bear with patience. The fact that knowledge is old and continues through the long ages is the chief reason for its contemporary importance.

For many years Professor McCrea has written in Latin the letters of greeting which Columbia University has offered to institutions of various sorts and kinds throughout the world when invited to participate in their official celebrations. He has discharged this scholarly task with a skill and a charm which are gratefully recognized and remembered by the entire University.

NICHOLAS MURRAY BUTLER

COLUMBIA UNIVERSITY IN THE CITY OF NEW YORK
 Commencement Day, June 2, 1936

CONTENTS

Portrait, from the Photograph by Underwood & Underwood Studios . . . . *Frontispiece*

LITERATURE AND LIBERALISM

LITERATURE AND LIBERALISM[1]

IN HIS PRESIDENTIAL ADDRESS to the American Historical Association in December, 1913, Professor William A. Dunning discussed with his wonted sagacity, moderation, and persuasive humor a certain characteristic of historical research during the last hundred years. He pointed out that during this period students of history had been chiefly concerned with the discovery of the things which had actually happened rather than with the causal nexus between these occurrences. " The absorbing and relentless pursuit of the objective fact " had thus become " the typical function of the modern devotee of history." In a most interesting and illuminating way Professor Dunning went on to point out that " the course of human history is determined no more by what is true than by what men believe to be true "; that " the phenomena of social life, so far as they are determined at all by the will of man, are due in origin and sequence to conditions as they appear to contemporaries, not to conditions as revealed in their reality to the historian centuries later "; and that, therefore, " we must recognize frankly that whatever a given age or people believes to be true, *is* true for that age and that people." It follows, then, that in the attempt to understand the course of events in their relations of cause and effect it is repeatedly the error and not the fact that is important.

In the presentation of this idea Professor Dunning

[1] Read at the annual meeting of the Classical Association of the Atlantic States at Philadelphia, April, 1916. Published in *The Columbia University Quarterly*, XIX (December, 1916).

drew some instances from the influence of Roman history in shaping the development of Europe, from the history of the Jewish nation as a factor in the life of Christendom, from the contribution made by the long credited relation between trial by jury and Magna Carta to the maintenance of constitutional government. His address was delivered before the outbreak of the present war. To anyone who is reasonably conversant with the enormous mass of apologetics which this war has called forth there can be, I think, no doubt that in any subsequent historical study of the causes of the conflict what the different governments and peoples believed to be true will be found to be far more relevant to an explanation of its origin than what really was true. Nor do I have any doubt that, if one considers with an open mind the records of universal history, he cannot escape the conclusion that the objective facts will but rarely be found adequate to account for their supposed effects. In other words, mankind always has clothed and always will clothe its perceptions of objective facts with its own feelings and beliefs, will always view these facts in the colors of its own predilections and prejudices, will in short seldom, if indeed ever except in rare individual instances, see these facts as they really are. Caesar, with characteristic insight into the infirmities of human nature, notes as one of the reasons for a decision of the Gauls *quod fere libenter homines id quod volunt credunt.*[2] And with reference to a wider sweep of thought, James Martineau in the preface to his fascinating book on *Types of Ethical Theory* acutely says: "Intellectual pride and self-ignorance alone can blind us to the fact that systems of philosophical opinion grow from the mind's instinctive

[2] *De Bello Gallico* iii. 18.

effort to unify by sufficient reason and justify by intelligible pleas its deepest affections and admirations." I wish, then, to draw at this point a conclusion of vital import to my subsequent argument, that all students of the activities of mankind, all those, in other words, who endeavor on any basis that is rational to deal with men as members of a social organism, must frankly admit that these activities and the ideas out of which they spring will not always, and probably will not even commonly, bear such a relation to the objective facts with which the ideas are concerned as to be predictable upon any knowledge of these facts alone. Such predictability, if there be any at all, must rest, in large measure, upon a study of human psychology in its weakness and capacity to misunderstand. And even so, there is multifarious evidence, supplied by the life of today no less than by the records of the past, that the vagaries of the human mind, or rather, perhaps, of the human heart, will constantly confound the purely rational observer. Even a dullard must observe that other people feel and reason differently both from himself and from one another in regard to the same things. But how few are so self-disciplined, how few have so far outgrown the self-confidence of the nursery, as to be led by their amusement at the obvious irrationality of their neighbors' views to ask themselves from the standpoint of an ideal observer whether their own views are not probably equally at variance with the same objective facts.

. . . . Quid rides? Mutato nomine de te
fabula narratur.[3]

In every life the principle of the personal equation is operative; in this respect each of us is necessarily

[3] Horace, *Satires* i. 1. 69, 70.

unus e multis. As Catullus, in a rare philosophic mood, aptly says:

> Nimirum idem omnes fallimur, neque est quisquam
> quem non in aliqua re videre Suffenum
> possis. Suus cuique attributus est error,
> sed non videmus manticae quod in tergo est.[4]

But the endeavor to comprehend in others and in our-selves also this *Suffenitas,* if you will permit me the word, is obligatory; for if we fail of this comprehension, we shall be unable to account for the sequence of events. Insularity can unfortunately coexist with great learning and even with great genius. Many persons of this dis-tinguished class thoroughly enjoy what Daniel Deronda so dreaded, " that dead anatomy of culture which turns the universe into a mere ceaseless answer to queries, and knows, not everything, but everything else about every-thing — as if one should be ignorant of nothing concern-ing the scent of violets except the scent itself for which one had no nostril." [5]

> Primroses by the river's brim,
> Dicotyledons were to him,
> And they were nothing more.

The group or class consciousness puts into fixed forms the standards of judgment and thus erects between man and man invisible, but almost impassable, barriers. François Villon in search of a lodging for the night has with the Seigneur de Brisetout that wonderful conversa-tion into which Stevenson has put all the pathos of a mutual incapacity to understand. But I need not enlarge further upon this point in either of its two aspects. The evidence is as the sands of the seashore for number. The elusiveness of the objective facts and the inability of

---

[4] 22. 18–21.   [5] George Eliot, *Daniel Deronda,* chap. xxxii.

those who in different and often contradictory ways are
equally astray in their conception of these facts to understand one another's language have been in the past among
the chief causes of the tragedy of human life. What of
the future?

Never, I suppose, has there been a time in the history
of the world when received opinions, however strongly
supported by long tradition, have been more called in
question. In every field of thought and investigation
critical scholarship is examining anew the bases of ortho-
doxy. The results of this destructive criticism are already
so striking that some of the ablest minds, ambitious of
an entire reconstruction of the world in terms of real
social justice, have gone so far as to regard the spirit
of conservatism as in itself the most serious enemy of
progress. But whatever might have been the outcome of
these critical processes under more normal conditions,
the great war has thrown a most lurid light upon our
supposed advance in civilization and has raised the gravest doubts as to the security of our position as heirs of
the ages. As Lord Bryce has said recently:

Sometimes one feels as if modern states were growing too huge
for the men to whom their fortunes are committed. Mankind in-
creases in volume, in accumulated knowledge, and in a comprehension of the forces of nature; but the intellects of individual men
do not grow. The disproportion between the individual ruling men
with their personal prejudices and proclivities, their selfish interests
and their vanities, and the immeasurable consequences which follow their individual volitions becomes more striking and more
tragic.

The long struggle for freedom of thought, so finely portrayed in Professor J. B. Bury's recent book, and for
that freedom of action through which alone freedom of
thought can be other than an academic idea, may after all

end in disaster. It would seem to be an appropriate time to ask again what ends education may serve and what elements may have most significance for the happiness of the race.

On the basis of the evidence afforded by not a few articles and books there are still in the world those who believe in war as a necessary element in man's spiritual growth. I have observed that no one of these thinkers has ever discussed what will happen if a single world-State or at least an amicable league of two or three huge States shall presently be evolved. As such conditions would on the basis of their own arguments insure peace, the human race would then, I suppose, begin to retrograde in civilization. However this may be, the thoughts of the world as a whole are now much concerned with the possibility of establishing some permanent basis of peace at the end of the present war. How may such a permanent basis be secured?

Let me call your attention at the outset to a few elementary considerations. You cannot by legislation make men good; you can at the best provide in this way a favorable environment. No law can be really enforced which does not have back of it the support of the community. Mankind is usually clever enough to find ways of evading a law in which it does not believe, and it will in case of necessity decline altogether to obey the law. It is a matter of common observation that, if the penalties imposed by a law are too severe, juries will not convict. If, then, we are to have peace in the years to come, if the widely differing ideas and ideals of individuals and nations are to have their fate determined by their own inherent vitality and not by external superior force, *an attitude of mind* must be produced which is friendly to such

liberty of growth, and hostile to limitation of the life of
ideas by the power and authority of stronger individuals
or stronger national organizations. To produce such an
attitude of mind among all men is a cardinal function of
education. To increase the number of those who think
and feel rationally and who are quite unwilling

> To prove their doctrine orthodox
> By Apostolic blows and knocks

must be one of the most important, if not, perhaps, in
any large way of considering the world's needs, the most
important of the results which any curriculum of study,
any scheme of education, must produce. I say *must;* for
it is evident that with the increasing mastery of man over
the secrets of nature, explosives and engines for their use
may easily be discovered in the future which will make
the instruments of destruction of the next great war as
much more deadly than those of today as those of today
are more deadly than the weapons of 1870. In such a
case the picture drawn by Mr. H. G. Wells in *The World
Set Free* might actually be realized.

What, then, if one considers the subject in the broadest
possible way, are the several educational factors which
may bring about such an attitude of mind? I shall attempt no invidious distinctions between the several
branches of knowledge. Each has its honorable function.
But there are three groups of studies which in definitely
larger measure than the rest seem likely to foster this
liberal spirit of which we have been speaking. These three
groups are: (1) mathematics and the natural sciences;
(2) the social sciences; (3) literature, philosophy, and
history. I am fully aware that the modern historian views
with distrust any association of history with literature,
but for our present purpose the old kinship still holds.

In effect, even if not with conscious intention, history, like philosophy, is concerned with the same end as literature. Let me at once define this end to be the interpretation of man to himself in such a moving and broadening fashion that his conception of the possibilities of his nature, of its many-sided capacity for new growth and new achievement, will make it difficult for him to be satisfied with a provincial outlook on this subject, or to rest content within fixed boundaries. The justice of this definition may well be called in question by one who considers only a single work, a single author, or even a single literary movement. But I am thinking rather of literature in its totality and of the determination of its inherent tendency from the evidence furnished by a comprehensive survey.

In every problem of education two elements are necessarily to be considered, man himself and his environment. This environment, in turn, is twofold: in part physical, subject to laws that are absolutely beyond his control; in part social, operating in any given form of society no less in conformity with law, but wearing a specious aspect of pliability. For as the laws of the social organism derive ultimately from the laws of his own nature and he seems to be a free agent, it is difficult to discover a necessary sequence of cause and effect. I yield to no one in my admiration for mathematics and the natural sciences. All the branches of knowledge in this first of our three groups involve the revelation of a majestic order in which there is no caprice neither shadow of turning; and so into the study of these branches — which alone seem to me to be in the strictest sense of the word true sciences — there has gone all of man's passionate longing for an invariant, eternal beauty of orderly structure in a world of which mutation and transitoriness seem to be the characteristic notes. Πάντα ρεῖ, as Heraclitus said. And men have sought for an escape from that truth into one transcending it. As Professor C. J. Keyser has finely expressed it:

Man contemplated as a spiritual being, as a thinker, poet, dreamer, as a lover of knowledge and beauty and wisdom and the joy of harmony and life, responding to the lure of an ideal destiny, troubled by the mysteries of a baffling world, conscious subject of tragedy, yearns for stable reality, for infinite freedom, for perpetuity and a thousand perfections of life.[6]

I yield delighted assent to the eulogy pronounced in this address on mathematics, and, by implication and in many cases by direct statement, on the natural sciences as well; but just because this eulogy is true in the terms which I have quoted, science, including mathematics, cannot be our chief aid in solving the particular problem which I have stated to you. This ordered universe of law in which cause produces effect in unbroken sequence represents to man a world into which he is slowly, as the centuries and millennia pass, educating himself, which ever beckons him onward, which affords to him in the midst of his feverish life a refreshing refuge, from which after a brief sojourn he may come back strengthened to face the almost insoluble problems of his daily existence. But these distressing problems which arise from the fact of his relations with his fellow men cannot be solved successfully by the temper of mind which is nourished by thoughts of invariance. It is the vagaries of human nature that are the causes of the difficulties; and every attempt to deal with human nature as if it were or could be static, or amenable except under duress to such con-

---

[6] "The Human Significance of Mathematics," in *The Human Worth of Rigorous Thinking* (Columbia University Press, 1916), p. 57.

trol as is essential in military discipline, will certainly in the end fail wholly.

It is indeed the distinguishing peculiarity of man that, product of his physical environment as he appears to be, he is nevertheless its superior and its judge. It is not from this environment that he draws his standards of perfection, but rather from the aspirations of his own nature.

> Laboriously tracing what must be
> And what may yet be better — [7]

he has always had visions of a world that would be " nearer to the heart's desire." He has in fact, as in the poetry of Shelley, given bodily form to such an ideal world, and pictured to himself how much more nobly life might there be ordered; and he must continue to be animated by this divine dissatisfaction under penalty of ceasing to be man and becoming simply an unreflecting part in the mechanism of the world machine. For this beautiful cosmic order, this passionless all-pervasive law, is essentially ruthless, and shows in its workings no kinship whatever with that moral sense for justice which is implicit in all human civilization. Nature, always " careless of the single life," is not always even " careful of the type," at least in the form which mankind regards as the noblest. And it is mankind, not Nature, that is the judge. As John Stuart Mill pointed out in his essay on " Nature,"

The only admissible moral theory of Creation is that the Principle of Good cannot at once and altogether subdue the powers of evil, either physical or moral; could not place mankind in a world free from the necessity of an incessant struggle with the maleficent powers or always make them victorious in that struggle; but could

[7] George Eliot, *The Choir Invisible.*

and did make them capable of carrying on the fight with vigour and with progressively increasing success.[8]

The study of the natural sciences is, then, indispensable. For they acquaint us with the conditions under which we are to fight, make clear the odds against us, and enable us to determine in what ways alone we may presently be victorious. But the object of the struggle is to make man the *master* of the forces of nature. Success is dependent upon exact knowledge, not easily or quickly to be acquired, of the sequences of cause and effect that obtain in nature's operations, sequences that are not only invariant but, *considered in themselves*, wholly amoral. It does not, therefore, seem reasonable that preoccupation with phenomena of this particular kind should fit one to be peculiarly helpful in the solution of problems which have their origin in the real or apparent clash of interests of fundamentally variable and moral beings.

One further fact is worthy of note. To the minds of scientists who are entirely great nothing can be called finally a scientific fact until, after it has been minutely investigated, verified, tested, and retested, it still yields always the same result. It thus attains the crowning hallmark of science, *i.e.*, impersonality and universal validity for mind *qua* mind. The true scientific temper is thus markedly cautious, and its possessor has no peculiar confidence in the final truth of his own personal theories. No one can read the *Life and Letters of Charles Darwin* without feeling the essential simplicity and modesty of his nature and the delicacy and winning power of his scientific doubt. But in minds of smaller caliber it must, I think, be admitted that scientific studies tend rather to foster than to moderate that confidence in the final

[8] " Nature," in *Three Essays on Religion* (Henry Holt & Co.), p. 45.

validity of one's own judgments which is the besetting infirmity of so many earnest and ambitious workers in every field of human activity. The imperious — and in itself wholly admirable — desire to be able to describe the facts of experience in terms of invariable sequences cannot well without strong reluctance admit the existence of definite limitations to its satisfaction. When one considers, for example, the brilliant discoveries of physico-chemical analysis, and the certain dependence of the life of organisms upon physical and chemical processes, it does not, perhaps, seem strange that the mechanistic explanation of the human mind has been by some scientists so confidently upheld. Yet it is increasingly clear, as Dr. J. S. Haldane has recently pointed out in his *Mechanism, Life and Personality,* that this conception has never been anything but " a working hypothesis of limited useful application." If, as many of us are still fain to believe, there is in man an incalculable element, if he is in reality forever rediscovering himself in terms of new experience, then no formulae of any kind involving invariable sequence will ever be adequate to describe his life, and there is need of the greatest caution lest science, to which he owes the priceless gift of liberation from superstition, may yet, at least for a season, persuade him that he is a link in a chain of material forces.

If mathematics and the natural sciences, invaluable as they are, will not provide for us precisely the help that we need, what shall we say of the social sciences? Just at this time these branches of knowledge stand in high favor. They are evidently mighty helpers in all noble endeavor to achieve a betterment of human life and of the conditions under which it is lived. They draw to their pursuit an increasingly large number of the most alert, ambitious, and high-minded of our students. Yet I cannot help thinking that these studies also leave something to be desired. The phenomena with which they deal have always been difficult to analyze. In our modern states with their huge populations, with political, industrial, and social organization of a bewildering complexity, it is extremely hard to distinguish the essential from the accidental and to arrive at a solution of a perplexing problem upon a basis that involves a permanent gain in comprehension of the issues involved. These sciences are perhaps as yet too young. Their results have not as yet been adequately expressed in forms of art. But their availability for the purposes of our present inquiry is certainly gravely impaired by their inherently administrative character. Concerned as they are with the quest for principles which will make it possible to organize human beings in the mass, and fully aware of the advantage to the individual of the collective activity of the community, these sciences tend to develop somewhat unduly belief in the efficacy of organization as such, and in their fine enthusiasm for the general gain tend to overlook the special claims of the individual. We have thus still to seek a corrective influence.

In the sense in which I am using the word in this inquiry literature is to be conceived, as I have already stated, as one of the means whereby man is made aware of the possibilities of his own nature and of that of his fellow men. Like all the fine arts, literature provides us with noble pleasure; but it finds its chief function as a criticism and interpretation of life. Its content, therefore, is the supremely important element. I am not forgetful of the doctrine of literary *genres* and of the historical evolution of these *genres* as part of the technique of the fine arts. But with reference to the function of literature of which I am speaking I should like to define style in a somewhat different way. The object of language is to convey thought and feeling from one mind to another without loss of moving power. Style, as it seems to me, is that form into which one may cast his conception with reasonable confidence that because of this form his conception will be able to operate without friction, *i.e.*, without loss of power. If in mechanics force be applied in an improper way, either the work will not be done at all, or, if done, will be accomplished only with a great waste of energy. If the style is adequate, the idea will have free play, and will even gain in power to move. But the supremely important thing is the human life itself that is thus adequately expressed. Of this portrayal the style is an inseparable part and not, as it were, a garment which may be donned or doffed. It can scarcely be a matter of doubt that if one studies literature in this way as the sublimated essence of the life of mankind, not ancient or medieval or modern literature, much less the literatures of separate countries, as, for example, Greece, Rome, France, Germany, England, Italy, America, if one studies rather world literature or any given section of the whole *as a section of the whole*, one will gain a very lively sense of the essential similarity of the problems that man has attempted to solve, of the very great difference of the solutions which have been advanced, and of the extraordinary diversity of small differences of detail which make each new form of the problem really after all a different problem. To put my meaning more clearly, the student of literature will find in its masterpieces, as he will not find in any of the natural sciences or in any of the social sciences, the imaginative portrayal of the inner life of man himself in connection with the problems that eternally imperil his happiness; and if such a student read with an open mind, he will presently become convinced that there has been no final solution because no final solution is possible. For it is the spiritual life of the race that is thus presented to his eyes, the concentration into a few score years of reading and reflection of the experience that might be gained by centuries of travel and intimate sympathetic companionship with myriad diverse types of self-expression, all described in forms of art by writers who themselves loved and understood the life they pictured. It would seem that no provincialism of outlook, no narrowness of social or political creed, no confidence in the absolute truth of one's own views, could fail in the end to succumb to such a many-sided intimacy with one's fellow beings. There can be no reasonable doubt that in the future as in the past human beings equally competent, equally sincere, equally high-minded, will answer the same question not only in different ways but even in antagonistic ways. For the clash of feeling and resultant action may arise from irreconcilable conceptions of the whole purpose of human life and of the part that it plays in the universe. How diverse are the worlds of Lucretius, Dante, and Goethe! Philosophers have come, have gone, and have been succeeded by others. Yet we are today no nearer a final solution of the mystery. Codes of ethics have met and are still today meeting with the same fate. The world still divides sharply as it has always done; and even where the old phrases are still employed, each new age reinterprets them to suit its own larger experience. Who shall decide these questions? Time possibly, but certainly no single age and still more certainly no single man, *e.g.*, the

reader of the tale at any given moment. Historical research has brilliantly shown that men and opinions may
be for generations treated in a manner far above or far
below their deserts. The judgment of contemporaries
does not necessarily prove anything. Centuries may pass
before justice is done — and justice may never be done.

What then is the lesson of literature for those who
would fain have peace in the world in the years to come?
It is essentially the same as the creed of liberalism; and
liberalism, we may note, is quite different from tolerance. As Mr. L. T. Hobhouse expresses it in *Liberalism:* [9]

The Liberal does not meet opinions which he conceives to be false
with toleration, as though they did not matter. He meets them with
justice and exacts for them a fair hearing as though they mattered
just as much as his own. He is always ready to put his own convic-
tions to the proof, not because he doubts them, but because he believes in them. For, both as to that which he holds for true and as
to that which he holds for false, he believes that one final test ap-
plies. Let error have free play, and one of two things will happen.
Either, as it develops, as its implications and consequences become
clear, some elements of truth will appear within it. They will separate themselves out; they will go to enrich the stock of human ideas;
they will add something to the truth which he himself mistakenly
took as final; they will serve to explain the root of the error; for
error itself is generally a truth misconceived, and it is only when it
is explained that it is finally and satisfactorily confuted. Or, in the
alternative, no element of truth will appear. In that case the more
fully the error is understood, the more patiently it is followed up
in all the windings of its implications and consequences, the more
thoroughly will it refute itself.

In the long run, unless we are willing to look forward to
a future of intermittent warfare, the intercourse of men
must be made to rest upon the basis of liberalism. Beyond question, situations will arise which will involve
very nice decisions, decisions about which there may be

[9] Pp. 116, 117.

considerable difference of opinion even among liberals; but here as in natural science experimentation will teach. Within reasonable limits of safety to the body politic and body social the widest and most varied laboratory work is desirable. However learned I may be, however expert in my field, I am not omniscient, nor can I possibly pronounce, as time perhaps will pronounce, upon the merit of a proposal in which I do not myself believe. Paradoxical as it may seem, if I am a sincere seeker for truth, I shall help my antagonist to put his case in the most favorable light and coöperate with him in securing an opportunity for putting his theory to the test. I shall do this because I am convinced that his theory will not work, and that the sooner it is demonstrated that it will not work, under conditions which he himself chooses as being especially favorable for success, the better for my own position.

At what, then, should we teachers of the classics aim, first, at all hazards, for ourselves, secondly, in such measure as may be possible, for our students. To put the answer briefly, the great authors — I beg you to note the adjective — the great authors, who because they possess the divining faculty of genius have something to say of permanent value on the philosophy and problems of human life, these great authors should be our intimate friends, known as such, as real personalities. There is a solidarity of mankind which transcends time and space. Despite all the difference between the ancient and the modern world, Plato speaks to us today no less intelligibly and with no less compelling power than John Stuart Mill, Vergil with no less power to make us feel the mystery of life than Wordsworth. Of this be sure: we may be able to translate our author, Lucretius, for instance, with

absolute correctness from cover to cover; we may have
at our fingers' ends the whole history of his text, his
sources, his peculiarities of diction and syntax. But if this
knowledge be, so to speak, dicotyledonous, if we do not
understand and appreciate in terms of life the meaning of
these facts, as an expression of the pathos of human life
and the saving power of reason by an extraordinary noble
and virile personality, then we shall miss the finest part
of the gift of literature. Others, but not we, shall know
Lucretius as a thoughtful friend, shall widen the circle by
including in it the other shining names of Greece and
Rome and their great successors in the centuries that
since have passed, and shall by daily intercourse with so
many-sided a company come into that largeness of vision
and wide sympathy which is real wisdom. And of wisdom
it is still true, as it was in the days of Solomon, that " her
ways are ways of pleasantness and all her paths are
peace."

*Iustitia est constans et perpetua voluntas ius suum
cuique tribuens.* Ulpian's conception of justice, repeated
in the opening words of the *Institutes* of Justinian, has
gained ground but slowly, as one may see, for example,
by considering the four thousand years of human activity
that have elapsed since the promulgation of the enlightened Code of Hammurapi. But, granted the presence of
the *voluntas,* actively *constans et perpetua,* there yet remains the all-important question, by whom the *ius
cuiusque* shall be defined, by the giver or by the receiver.
From this root have sprung those countless conflicts in
which with the noblest intentions men have granted, or
rather imposed, a *ius* which the recipients passionately
rejected. Always there has been too much at work that
naïve understanding of the Golden Rule which leads A

scrupulously to give to B (whose ideals are quite different from A's) what A himself would desire to receive if he (still unchangeably A) were in B's situation. *Voilà la comédie humaine — tragique!* For B, having achieved his *ius* as he himself defines it, proceeds then to deal with C (who agrees with neither A nor B) in precisely the same spirit in which A has dealt with him. Few, indeed, have been the successful rebels against constraint who have not in turn been eager to constrain. But literature, which is the mirror of life and therefore of man's infinite variety, will yet with the help of philosophy and history — for the help of these two disciplines is indispensable for the full comprehension of the portrayal — make it clear to every open mind that the individual does not and cannot acquiesce in another's definition of his *ius,* and that in the future control must be exercised rather over the conditions amid which he develops his personality than over this development itself. For personality can no more be permanently enchained than could Proteus of old.

LATIN LITERATURE[1]

IT HAS BEEN commonly recognized that Latin literature has two distinct claims upon the attention of the modern mind. It records on the one hand the interpretation of human life reached by a great nation, whose disciplined bravery conquered the known world and whose juristic and administrative genius then slowly worked out the idea of a single imperial nationality for all the diverse peoples of its wide domain. This conception of the possible political unity of mankind, first partially and but momentarily realized in the empire of Alexander the Great, was discerned again by Polybius as he sought to understand the reasons why in half a century the civilized world had fallen under the sway of Rome. In the train of conquest followed organization, and with two exceptions, the Greek and the Jew, ultimate assimilation. A common language sufficiently flexible to adjust itself to the new demands made upon it, a common law whose development had long been profoundly influenced by the Stoic doctrine of an eternal law of nature superior in its authority to any specific human legislation, the movements of trade and commerce made possible by the widespread *pax Romana*, all tended to bind closely together the manifold elements of the Empire. Caracalla's extension of Roman citizenship to all free inhabitants of the Roman world, though not so intended, was but a natural recognition of existing conditions. "The Syrian, the Pannonian, the Briton, the

1 Reprinted from *Lectures on Literature* (Columbia University Press, 1911).

Spaniard, called himself a Roman." [2] And presently with this idea of a civil unity there came to be most intimately associated the idea of a religious unity, so that for centuries the belief in the eternal existence of the Church carried with it as a necessary consequence a belief in the endless duration of the Empire. For thousands of human beings Rome thus came to be a spiritual idea rather than a definitely localized city. Strange, indeed, it would be if the literature of a nation so virile, so constructive, whose career determined the whole subsequent course of Western European history, were not at least sufficiently expressive of the national genius to command our most serious consideration.

But there is another aspect of Latin literature of the greatest historical importance. It was Rome that assimilated and transmitted to the Western World the culture of Greece. During those five hundred years in which the city on the Tiber gradually fought her way from the position of a struggling little community in the midst of menacing neighbors to the assured control of the whole Italian peninsula, the Greeks, already possessed of their Homer, invented and brought to perfection in various parts of the Greek-speaking world the fundamental types of literary expression in poetry and in prose. It was practically inevitable that when, upon the conquest of Magna Graecia and through the later wars in Greece and in the Hellenized East, the ruling class at Rome became acquainted with the masterpieces of Greek art and letters, captive Greece should, in Horace's phrase, take captive her rude conqueror. A generation succeeded whose education from youth up was full of Greek influences. The younger Scipio Africanus, a man of wonderful ability,

[2] James Bryce, *The Holy Roman Empire,* chap. ii.

many-sidedness, and taste, possessed of a most winning personality, became the leader of a circle of statesmen and writers who were confident of the nation's future, enthusiastic over the new culture, and convinced that the language might most surely and most swiftly be molded into the medium for a great national literature by the close study of Greek models. The tide of Hellenism came to its flood in the prose of Cicero and the poetry of Vergil, the one the most widely cultivated mind of all antiquity, the other, in Bacon's words, " the chastest poet and royalest that to the memory of man is known," and both, in the influence which they exerted alike upon the minds of the generations which immediately followed them and in the intellectual life of Western Europe since the Renaissance, as all-pervasive as Latinity itself. The unity of the Empire and the ease of communication between its parts led to the wide diffusion of this Graeco-Roman culture throughout the provinces. It was an integral element in the life of the new nationalities, and even the reëntrance upon the scene in the fifteenth century of the Greek originals themselves failed to deprive it of its primacy as a formative power. It was still the Latin writers who were models of style and whose ideas swayed the development of art and letters. Not until the eighteenth century did Greek come really into its own.

One of the fruits of the nineteenth century was the formulation and wide application of the historical and comparative method in the study of all the results of human activity. To the investigators and critics who thus followed the stream of literature back to its fountain heads this second aspect of Latin literature seemed to be of paramount significance. The unquestioned indebtedness of Rome to Greece in all the technique of form, the constant

and, at times, even minute use by the Latin writers of the
rich material gathered in the earlier literature seemed to
these students to make Latin at the best but a pale and
ineffectual reflex of the Greek. But already there is evidence that a different and saner view will presently obtain. It is being pointed out that we cannot thus estimate
Latin literature without including in the same con-
demnation much of that which is most justly admired in
our modern literatures. When once the literary types
have been worked out, there remains but one possible
originality, an originality of personality and spirit. Man
is inevitably the heir of the ages, and " with the process
of the suns " the elements for which he is indebted to the
past become as inevitably ever more and more numerous.
Even the *Iliad* is now recognized to be a highly artificial
production and to presuppose a long anterior period of
poetic activity. It has been proven again and again, as,
for instance, in the case of the plots of Shakespeare's
plays, that a poet may borrow material from others without in any way impairing his own claim to eminent or
even preëminent merit. For the supreme test of a great
work of art must be found in its unfailing power to give
noble pleasure to minds that are sensitive to such beauty,
and not in the answer to the question whether the artist
has taken from existing sources the material into which
he has himself put this subtle magic. Judged by such a
standard rather than by that of their genetic relation to
their predecessors, the place of the names that are the
glory of Latin literature may be regarded as having long
since been fixed by the consensus of opinion of successive
generations. More than this, recent studies are revealing
with increasing clearness that, while not only in form and
rhythm but also (especially in the case of the poets) in

idea, phrase, and color they drew freely upon their models, the spirit and total effect of their work is essentially Roman, not Greek. With some striking exceptions, chiefly in the field of the drama, this work reflects the environment of the writer, social, political, or religious, and gives expression to the spirit of the time, its moods, gay or severe, its aspirations, self-criticism, or despair. Naevius and Ennius both fought for Rome in the field before they composed their national epics. *Horace,* in the opinion of a distinguished French critic, M. Pierron, *est, si je l'ose ainsi dire, le siècle d'Auguste en personne.*[3] The appeal of Vergil's *Aeneid* to his countrymen was so immediate that to them not Aeneas but the Roman people itself was the real hero. We walk the very streets of Rome and note the manners of the passing throng with Juvenal and Martial. Even Lucretius, who seems so detached a personality, and who is so proud, after the manner of all true Epicureans, of his absolute dependence upon the scrolls of his revered master, produced a poem which is, as Professor John Veitch said some time ago, " a type in the world of thought of the irrepressible Roman spirit of absolute sovereignty and love of orderly rule in the world of practical life and action." [4] And this Roman spirit shows itself not only in the conquering toil with which the masses of disparate phenomena that prove to him the invariable order of natural law are finally marshaled in a coherent and interrelated series of arguments, but even more in the manner and temper with which this result is achieved. The literary movement of the time was already Alexandrine, with its love of carefully polished work in miniature, learned, romantic, and sentimental. But from

---

[3] *La Littérature romaine,* pp. 404, 405.
[4] *Lucretius and the Atomic Theory,* p. 13.

the group of young poets of this school to which Catullus, Calvus, and Cinna belonged, Lucretius stood quite aloof. To his eager mind, intensely absorbed in the presentation of that philosophy which would insure in every recipient soul the dethronement of illusion, the reign of reason, most of their work must have seemed mere studied prettiness. How should a poet whose verse reveals an instinctive sympathy with forces that operate on a grand scale in illimitable space and in unending time concern himself with the ephemeral passions and ambitions of the moment? Catullus himself, who immortalizes this moment, was possessed of too vigorous, too Roman, a temperament to be fettered by his Alexandrian technique. Impassioned alike in love and in hate, whether personal or political, he uses a diction extraordinarily lucid and direct. In the longer elegies and in the epyllion on the *Marriage of Peleus and Thetis* there is unmistakable evidence of deliberate art and even artifice. But in the poems that are expressive of his own feeling — and no poet is more egoistic — there is a spontaneity which cannot be matched in any other Latin poet, and the verse is most exquisitely adapted to the shifting phases of emotion.

The poem of Lucretius is in another way characteristically Roman. Epicurus had indeed " traversed throughout in mind and spirit the immeasurable universe whence he returns victorious to tell us what can, what cannot come into being — on what principle each thing has its powers defined, its deepset boundary mark." But this quest had not been undertaken through any desire to enlarge the boundaries of science for its own sake. He had, on the contrary, a social aim, to secure the necessary foundation for the most indispensable and universal of all arts, the art of living. Such knowledge as was con-

tributory to this end was of vital importance; all else
might, at the best, serve to amuse an idle hour. In this
limitation Epicurus is in no wise distinctively Greek. But
with the normally constituted Roman the question of the
practical results of his labors was always primary. Like
Mr. Kipling's typical American, he turned his face naturally to " the instant need of things " and turned it too
with much the same " keen, untroubled " gaze. Horace,
in the Epistle to Augustus in which he champions the
modern school of Latin poetry as against the indis-
criminate laudation of the classic dead, makes at one
point a defense of poetry itself on purely utilitarian
grounds. With characteristic irony, but in full appreciation of the current standard of value, he claims that the
poetic temperament brings in its train many practical ad-
vantages. The poet is, at least, apt to be free from many
common faults : —

> Rarely does avarice taint the tuneful mind.

And in all seriousness he does good service to the State.
In the education of the young and the comforting of the
old, in the commending of a noble yet practicable rule of
life, in the worship that wins for man the favor of heaven,
the poet plays a part that must secure him against the
criticism of being a drone in the busy hive.

Cicero, too, found it necessary to justify on like
grounds his interest and work in philosophy. That delight in the intellectual life for its own sake, that passion
for inquiry and knowledge as the natural food of the human mind which Cicero so enthusiastically describes in
a great passage in the last book of his *De Finibus*,[5] was by
no means native in the Roman mind, and to the majority

[5] v. 48–54.

always appeared to be a vain thing. One recalls with amusement the story told about the proconsul Gellius, a contemporary of Cicero. This progressive governor, with a love of order truly and admirably Roman, called before him upon his arrival at Athens the representatives of the various schools of philosophy and, urging upon them the propriety of making a final adjustment of their differences, offered in perfect good faith his service as mediator.[6] Panaetius, the friend of the younger Scipio, and by far the most influential of all Greek thinkers in winning converts to Stoicism at Rome, gained his success by emphasizing, not the lofty but wholly theoretical conception of virtue held by the earlier Stoics, but an ideal which might be realized in actual life. The new doctrine found congenial soil, for the heroes of Roman tradition were, as has been pointed out, unconscious Stoics. It was found that this view of life, in its idea of a world order to which the individual was bound to conform, in its treatment of the deities of popular belief as manifestations of the one Divine Being, in its insistence on the duties which every man owed to society and the State, was in essential harmony with some of the strongest elements in the national character. This theory could be definitely helpful in solving the problems of daily life. It might be used to reinforce the constraining power of the *mos maiorum,* as this was still felt in the organization of the family and the State. And if presently " the way of the fathers " should cease to be able to provide adequate sanction for personal and civic morality (the Empire saw this danger realized in the extinction of liberty), philosophy might take its place altogether in maintaining the standard. Cicero is much concerned to make clear this practical value of his

---

[6] Cicero, *De legibus* i. 53.

own labors in this field, to relate them not so much to human life in general as to the particular needs of his countrymen and their historical traditions, to show that because of the discipline and breadth which it alone could give the study of philosophy was for a self-governing people, and especially for the statesman and the publicist, a necessary complement of the regular training in literature, law, and oratory. In the series of volumes which appeared in rapid succession in the years 45 and 44 B.C., dealing in part with the criterion of knowledge, in part with the ethical standard, Cicero was, he conceived, meeting a practical need as certainly as in his earlier works on rhetoric and political science.

One of these earlier works, the treatise *On the State*, has come down to us in a very fragmentary condition, but enough remains to enable us to form a definite idea of Cicero's political philosophy. The book offers a most instructive contrast to the famous *Republic* of Plato on which Cicero modeled his own work. The aim of both inquirers is substantially the same; namely, to ascertain the moral principles of an ideal polity and to describe its governmental form. But the earlier thinker, approaching the problem in the spirit of a speculative philosopher in search of the absolute good, works out with inflexible logic the consequences of that principle of justice which must be realized both in the State and in its citizens. The result is the construction of a marvelously intricate and interrelated social organism, a book crowded with ideas and ideals of permanent value. But the State, as specifically constituted, is wholly theoretical, at variance with all human experience, and incapable of realization. The Roman, though he has a most engaging enthusiasm for great ideas, is far too completely the child of his race

to put any faith in a series of abstract ethical propositions and their necessary corollaries. He, too, describes
an ideal State, but he is evidently, after all, idealizing
an actually tested form of government: namely, the
constitution of Rome as it existed in the time of the
younger Scipio Africanus. He would fain in his own age
have played the part of a Laelius to the Scipio of Pompey, and, as he looked back to those golden days, so different from the lowering present, it seemed to him that
Polybius was right in thinking that Rome then possessed " the most beautiful framework of government of
all that are in our times known." [7]

Important as it was in Cicero's judgment that his
countrymen should be made familiar with the subject
matter of Greek philosophy, it was no less important
that these ideas should be presented in a style that would
serve both to win for them a readier hearing and to enrich the literature with an artistic form not hitherto
represented. The undertaking bristled with difficulties.
There was as yet in existence in Latin no treatment of
philosophy in prose of the slightest scientific or literary
value. Lucretius indeed had lived; but his work was in
poetry, and dealt with one single school of thought and
in the main with only one aspect, the physical and
mechanical, of the teaching of even that school. It was
necessary to create a philosophical vocabulary; and,
while even the plastic Greek had only in the hands of
a long succession of thinkers become wholly adequate
for the expression of abstract thought, Latin, a language which finds perhaps the most striking monu-
ment of its purely native capacity in the objective con-
creteness of Caesar's *Commentaries*, had to be made

---

[7] Polybius vi. 10. 14. See Cicero, *De re publica* i. 70.

through the genius of a single worker an instrument of like power. The notable success which was achieved would no doubt have been impossible if Cicero had not profited to the utmost by the terminology already worked out in Greek. Even so considered, it was an amazing feat, the far-reaching importance of which did not appear until long after his death. For, as the event proved, it was Cicero who made possible the Latinity of the Church Fathers from Minucius Felix to Saint Augustine, and to whom the scholastic philosophy of the Middle Ages owed the medium requisite for its expression.

Whence came this marvelous power over language, which from the days of Quintilian, his ardent admirer, made Cicero the most potent influence in Roman education, which in the Renaissance captivated Petrarch, and, through that great movement in which Petrarch was the pioneer, placed Cicero in his commanding position as a literary artist? The answer must be found in the development of oratory at Rome. In Tacitus's *Dialogue* on this subject, it is pointed out in defense of the oratory of the Republic and of Cicero as its greatest representative that "it may be said of eloquence, as of a flame, that it requires motion to excite it, fuel to feed it, and that it brightens as it burns." [8] For "the mental powers of the orator rise with the dignity of his subject and no one can produce a noble and brilliant speech unless he has an adequate case." [9] As Tacitus was only too well aware, great eloquence is most intimately connected with the vigor and freedom of national life. When that life is instinct with great ideas and principles, when the minds and passions of men are deeply stirred by political and social movements of grave import to the commonwealth,

[8] 36.　　　　[9] 37.

the conditions are most favorable for a native eloquence, and, if training be added, for a great style. In the survey of the development of Roman oratory which Cicero has given to us in the *Brutus,* it is clear that, from the day when Appius Claudius Caecus made against the conclusion of a peace with Pyrrhus the first published speech in Roman annals, the fiercely disputed questions of internal and foreign policy and the sessions of the law-courts resulted in a continuous improvement of a practical art that was most congenial to the Roman temperament. The elder Cato, Gaius Gracchus, Crassus and Antonius, the teachers of Cicero in his youth, Hortensius, his great rival at the bar, " the king of the courts," mark the steps of a progress from rude natural effectiveness to artistic excellence that we can ourselves trace even in the tantalizingly few fragments of their speeches which have been preserved. With Cicero our data become abundant, for there are extant fifty-seven of more than one hundred speeches which he delivered. These speeches, studied in connection with his masterly treatises on the ideal orator, prove that not only did he bring Latin prose style to the highest point of formal development, but also that in one very real sense he may actually be called its founder. The earlier orators, it is true, had learned much from Greek rhetoricians, alive and dead, about the harmony which should exist between form and content, but Cicero was the first to work out and to use on a large scale a comprehensive theory of oratory as a fine art, in so far as it might be capable of realization in Roman life and in the Latin tongue. This theory was the slow fruition of close study of Greek masters and masterpieces, and he is peculiarly indebted to Isocrates, to whom, in fact, in Greek literature also all subsequent prose writers were ultimately indebted for the rhythmical swell of the periodic sentence. By the most intense and unremitting application, by the devotion of a lover to his art, Cicero made himself a consummate master of rhetorical structure, of phrase, and of cadence. Neither Flaubert nor Stevenson ever worked more passionately than he to achieve style, to cast his thoughts into such a form as to satisfy at once the critical mind and the critical ear. The prose which he thus perfected was naturally the prose of the orator, the prose of one who addressed an actual audience. When later he began to adapt it to meet the needs of the treatise and the essay, it was still a prose that was shaped to yield its meaning and its charm on the first reading. In fact, even those of his works that were intended to be read rather than to be heard are cast in the form of the dialogue. The same tone naturally appears in his *Letters*. Their vivacity and changing moods reproduce the movement of animated conversation, and in nothing that he has left to us is the sureness and ease of his control of the language more striking. His correspondents, men of distinction though they were, fall markedly below his level.

In that dialogue of Tacitus to which I have already referred, it is claimed by the admirer of the republican oratory that, " while the style of Caesar is the more transparent, the style of Cicero is the more impassioned, the richer, the more forcible." [10] As none of Caesar's speeches has survived, we have no means of verifying the estimate of Cicero, who places him in the very first rank, but we are probably justified in forming some idea of the secret of his success through his *Commentaries* on the Gallic and Civil wars. These " materials for the study of his-

[10] 25.

tory " are presented in a manner that, for its purity of idiom, lucidity, and terseness, is, as Cicero says in the *Brutus,* the despair of professed historians.[11] Still, unadorned as is the style, the sentences flow and are woven together into a continuous web. But already a different ideal of writing had found its great representative. Historical composition had begun at Rome with the *Origins* of the elder Cato, whose motto had been " make sure of the sense, and the words will follow." The practical value of history was evident to the Roman mind, and this field was accordingly much cultivated. Under the Empire, indeed, the historians became the foremost representatives of prose. But historiography developed slowly; and Sallust, contemporary with Cicero and Caesar, was the first to use a scientific method and an artistic form. Attracted by Thucydides rather than by Isocrates, he worked out a new type of Latin prose style, highly compressed in thought and in expression, abrupt and epigrammatic. He is a lover of the words and phrases of a bygone age, with a special fondness for Cato. His sentences, for the most part short and simple in their structure, follow one another staccato fashion. Quintilian speaks admiringly of his " immortal swiftness." It is a style quite conscious of its own art, which it by no means attempts to conceal. Next to Cicero, Sallust is the chief model in prose for the following centuries. Tacitus learned of him, and still later, in an archaizing age, he is highly regarded by Fronto and by Gellius.

The two fundamentally opposed ideals of form which came to expression in the prose of Cicero and of Sallust, respectively, were destined to receive under the Empire a most characteristic and most splendid realization in the

[11] 262.

historical work of two geniuses of the first rank. The governing factor in the development of republican prose had been the need, imperative in spoken discourse, of being understood at once, as the words succeeded one another. The style had to be fused with the thought, and, like it, had to be such as to win instant appreciation. But with the loss of freedom and the decline of oratory conditions changed. The appeal was then made even more to a reading than to a listening public. The gentle reader might linger over the art of the writer, and this art in turn might be made so intricate in its nice balance of phrase and clause, so daring in the compactness of its thought and structure, so subtly suggestive in the literary associations of its diction, as to reveal its full charm and power only after some attentive consideration. It is in this fashion that Livy continues the Ciceronian tradition, and Tacitus the Sallustian. The two men are as far apart in temperament and method as they are different in manner. Judged by modern standards, Livy is in no sense a scientific historian. To examine, whenever possible, original sources, to sift with a critical and open mind a mass of conflicting evidence, to search for the truth with an austere disregard of the possible resultant destruction of one's own cherished opinions, all this was alien to his enthusiastic soul. He never consciously misrepresents the facts, but he is essentially a hero worshiper, and his greatest hero is the Roman Commonwealth itself. "Fallen on evil times," as he thinks, he idealizes the great past, and, conceiving, as we read in his famous preface, that it is the function of history to teach good citizenship, he is unconsciously predisposed to accept that form of the story which will enable him to point his moral most effectively. Yet such is his innate sympathy and kinship with the elements of character which made Rome great that, notwithstanding grave deficiencies, his work has an enduring truth and value. It is really a prose epic, written in a style of extraordinary eloquence and picturesqueness. To the historian and to the lover of literature alike the loss of more than three-quarters of the entire work is certainly the greatest which Latin literature has sustained.

A great modern historian, Leopold von Ranke, says of Tacitus: " If one yields to the impression made by his works, one is carried away by it. There is no trace in him of the manner and method of Greek historiography. He is Roman through and through, and indeed the master of all who have written before or since." Unlike Livy, Tacitus brought to the help of his historical investigation the practical training gained in a long and distinguished official career. In the opening paragraphs of the *Histories* and the *Annals* he avows his intention to write with perfect freedom from prejudice. A thorough aristocrat and lover of the old order, he saw, nevertheless, that the Empire was definitively established. He could even fully appreciate the enlightened rule of a Trajan. But the fifteen years of " silent servitude " under Domitian had permanently embittered his soul, and despite his best efforts the prevailing somberness of his thoughts profoundly influenced his judgment as a historian. Though by no means unerring in his analysis, he was endowed by nature with a marvelous power to trace the hidden springs of thought and action. His portrayal of character is subtle and vivid. The phrases bite as does the acid in etching. The style is charged with imagination, and everywhere in the diction one sees the influence of Vergil, to whom alike as artist and as patriot his own personality was so closely akin.

Nothing in the whole range of Latin literature illustrates more strikingly its close connection with the national character and the need of the time than the work of Rome's greatest poet. The long years of civil strife that terminated in the battle of Actium had exhausted Italy, had substituted factional bitterness for the sense of a common country and had made of slight effect the traditional moral and religious sanctions of civic conduct. Augustus and his ministers, confronted by the urgent need of reconstruction, called into play remedial forces of very varied kinds. Among these was literature. Vergil's *Georgics* is not a poem born of the love of Nature for her own sake, though Vergil shows such love, nor does it treat of the life of man in the country in any cosmopolitan way. Italy is the theme, and the Roman virtues and strength of character fostered by the hard struggle with the reluctant yet bountiful earth. For agriculture was, if possible, to be again honorably esteemed, as in the days when Cincinnatus left his plow to guide the State. The poem is the quintessence of long musing on the subject in one of the loveliest parts of Italy and of a study of the effects of word and phrase that was almost microscopic. The fruit of seven full years of labor was a poem of 2,200 lines — less, on the average, than a line a day. But this poem at once made its author the object " of a people's hope." And this hope was justified in the *Aeneid*. Here Vergil shows himself to be one of that very small number of poets who appeal to the universal heart of man. No other poem in the world's literature is more many-sided, no other has played so large a part in the

mental life of so many generations of men. Yet Vergil
was far from consciously writing for any such audience.
He " sounds forever of Imperial Rome," whose finer life
he strove adequately to express and to quicken. Possessed
in the highest degree of that catholic receptivity which
both Polybius and Posidonius noted as among the admirable qualities of the Roman mind, he used as by
natural right the imaginative interpretation of human
life of his great predecessors, whether Greek or Roman.
But he puts upon all the stamp of his own personality,
essentially Roman in his purpose and totality of effect,
even where the material is most Homeric.

" Our wills are ours, to make them Thine." It would
be impossible to define here the full significance of the
Aeneid. Professedly a poem of action, it is in fact a musing upon the mystery of human life, upon its infinite
pathos, its uncertain issue, its permitted greatness. To
the modern world, with its apotheosis of the individual
man, Aeneas, as Vergil has drawn him, is apt to seem
rather a concept than a real human being. Yet he incarnates the virtues upon which, to the poet's mind, depended the realization of the high hopes of the new order.
The age had learned to its cost the meaning of personal
ambition. Vergil held up to it the contrasted picture of
patience, self-control, and obedience to the divine call.
Through such forgetfulness of self, and through this
alone, it had been possible to lay the foundations of the
State ; through the same high devotion Rome had grown
great. In no other way could her life be preserved and
enriched for the generations to come.

Horace, Vergil's contemporary, is in another way
equally the child of his age and responsive to the movement of the time. Between the Homeric Odysseus and the

Vergilian Aeneas, says Sainte-Beuve, "*l'urbanité était née*." [12] Horace, as ready in his address as Vergil was shy and awkward, is, in a special sense, the representative in Latin literature of this temper and manner. It is not, of course, peculiar to his works. We admire it also, for instance, in the distinguished Romans who figure in Cicero's dialogue *On the Orator*. In the poet's familiar *Talks* and *Letters* we are listening to an accomplished man of the world. Fully aware of the difficulties which beset the pathway of life, he criticizes with kindly humor and tolerance the foibles and errors of others, and derives from his own an amusement which he shares with his readers. Yet, with all this gaiety of tone, he pursues, true Roman that he is, a very practical end: namely, the determination of the principles by which one may order one's life aright. The teaching of the schools gave him, no doubt, greater breadth of view, but Horace's philosophy of life is ultimately the outcome of that habit of shrewd observation of courses of action and their results which his father had so sedulously fostered. It finds expression even in his lyric poetry, on which his fame as a great literary artist chiefly rests. "The light that never was on sea or land" comes not to him. But if, even in the *Odes,* we have "the light of common day," it is none the less a world touched with the hues of fancy and with man's finer tastes and hopes. Like Vergil, he is in full sympathy with the efforts of the new régime to restore the ideals of the past. The noble series of odes that opens the third book is in effect a single poem in which Horace commends "*virginibus puerisque*" the moral qualities that should be theirs, both as individuals and as citizens of Rome.

[12] *Étude sur Virgile*, p. 243.

The marked peculiarity of Roman constitutional history [says Professor James S. Reid] is its unbroken evolution, whereby a mode of government which originally sprang up in connection with a small town community was gradually adapted for the direction of a widespread empire. No violent breach of continuity is to be found in the whole course of the changes which passed over the political existence of Rome from the dawn of its history to its latest phases.[13]

One may and one should, I think, find in Latin literature the reflection of the same continuously developing national life. A number of instances have been discussed to show the intimate relation that existed between these two things. But a few cases only have been taken out of a possible many. One might go farther and point out how in the early days of the literature the rollicking fun and wit of Plautus assume forms which could not possibly have been derived from his Greek originals and whose spirit is truly Italian; how Terence gave to the still undisciplined language a polish that delighted even the critical taste of the Ciceronian age and justly prided himself upon being a well of " Latin undefiled." One might note the brilliancy with which Ovid's verse mirrors the gay, cultivated, and cynical society of the world's capital in the beginning of the Imperial era. Juvenal's pitiless indictment of his time must be corrected by the cheerful optimism of the younger Pliny, who is as circumstantial in his praise of the persons and things that were good as is Juvenal in his indignation with the persons and things that were evil. And so one might deal with many a name. The language, too, shows a homogeneous growth from the writers of the third century before Christ to Boëthius in the sixth century A.D. Inherently sonorous and digni-

[13] " The Roman Constitution," in *A Companion to Latin Studies,* Edited by J. E. Sandys, p. 243.

fied, inherently logical in the structure of its sentences, as, for instance, in the predominating use of the principle of subordination as against that of coördination, it reflects in point after point the mental traits of the people that used it. If it is ever true that *le style est l'homme même,* then one must see in the Latin language and its literature the unmistakable impress of the race whose consummate genius was for law and order and government.

Tu regere imperio populos, Romane, memento —
Hae tibi erunt artes — pacisque imponere morem,
Parcere subiectis et debellare superbos.[14]

[14] Vergil, *Aeneid* vi. 851–53.

HUMANISM, OLD AND NEW:
LUCRETIUS AND HORACE[1]

I AM TO SPEAK to you this evening and, if your kindly
interest extends so far, next Monday evening as well on
" Humanism, Old and New." It is a theme long dear to
my heart, a theme indeed which, though it makes its special appeal to all of us who love the studies that are called
the " humanities," cannot but receive from the scientist
also, at least in his philosophic moods, most serious consideration. For, however variously humanism may be
defined, there is always involved in it the appraisal of
moral and esthetic values. Whether his thoughts be concerned with literature, the fine arts, the natural sciences,
or the social sciences, the humanist should not merely
know and understand human achievement in relation to
the civilization out of which it sprang, but also — and this
is imperative — he should determine the worth and significance of it for human life, see things in perspective,
analyze and interpret recorded experience to the end that
mankind may be able to realize more and more adequately its desire to live a worthy life. Scientists, as such,
are subject to no such obligation. Their business is to
assemble data, to correlate and explain these data, and
thus to make possible on the one hand a better understanding of the activities of nature's marvelous workshop,
and on the other, a series of new inventions for the use of
mankind. This use is not in every instance necessarily

[1] The first of two public lectures delivered at Columbia University in March,
1932; the second is omitted here because it is to form part of a volume on
Cicero's philosophy.

beneficent. Explosives may be employed for opposite purposes. The skill into which exact knowledge of the energies and processes of nature may be transmuted is simply
a means to an end, a tool which is equally at the service
of the saint and the sinner, of the altruist and the self-
seeker. This obvious fact, all-important for the humanist,
is for the scientist a matter of no concern whatever. Yet
even he is a human being, not solely a research worker
and inventor; and in intervals of leisure he too will muse
upon the realization by mankind of a life commensurate
with the dignity of those who belong to the *genus homo,*
and will be proud of the priceless help which science has
given toward making that vision a reality.

But the word " humanism," like all general terms, has
in actual practice been used to describe widely differing
phases of one general attitude of mind. In a famous essay [2] John Stuart Mill discusses the confusion of thought
and feeling caused by the widespread use of the terms
" nature " and " natural " without close attention to the
very different meanings which, in the course of time,
these words and their kin have developed; and with his
usual crystalline clarity shows how this confusion has
become the source of false taste, false philosophy, false
morality, and even bad law. Prudence therefore suggests
and the shortness of the time at our command requires
a delimitation of the scope of our inquiry. It is certainly
difficult, if not impossible, to frame a single comprehensive definition of humanism. The concepts that have
come to be associated with it are too many and too diverse. The men of the Renaissance who were first described by the word " humanist " lived very different
lives. As Professor Frank J. Mather, Jr., has recently

[2] " Nature," in *Three Essays on Religion* (Henry Holt & Co.), pp. 3–65.

pointed out,[3] these seekers after an autonomous and many-sided personal culture made very different uses of their precious acquisitions.

Some, like Sir Thomas More, Aeneas Sylvius Piccolomini, Lorenzo the Magnificent, applied their culture to public affairs. Others, like Petrarch and Erasmus, viewed the world from afar as secluded men of letters and detached critics. Some, like the tender-minded neo-Platonist Pico della Mirandola, lived on ideal heights of intuition. . . . Most of them were in their own fashion religious, but their faith ran from the mystic faith of a Marsilio Ficino and the hearty piety of a Colet to the decent conformity of the skeptic Montaigne and the thin, if lofty, Deism of Leonardo da Vinci.

But all these different personalities turned to classical antiquity for inspiration. If, accordingly, we add to the famous names associated with the Revival of Learning the great poets, philosophers, and historians of Greece and Rome, artists who were profoundly humanistic though the term had not been coined to designate them as such, we shall be embarrassed by the richness and diversity of our material, even if we take no account at all of those who in our own time would fain be classed as humanists. Thus constrained, I have chosen for your consideration three representatives, all Roman, but nevertheless unlike in type: Lucretius, essentially a student, analyst, and spectator of life, whose outlook on humanity is so Olympian in its breadth, so detached in its intense sympathy, that even the greatness of the imperial city is rarely present in his thoughts, who seems to have been as little concerned with the momentous political movements of his age as Goethe was with Napoleon's ambitions at the time of the battle of Jena; Horace, in his youth an ardent defender on the battlefield of Philippi of

[3] "Humanism — Attitude or Credo?", *Atlantic Monthly,* June, 1930, p. 741.

a great political tradition, then in sore peril, in middle life an earnest but sober-minded supporter in lyrical verse (notably in the six national Odes at the beginning of Book III) of the state policies of the shrewd and able leader against whom he had earlier taken up arms, keenly interested in the social and political changes of his time but never disposed to serve as a member of a civic committee to bring any particular change to pass, tireless in his endeavor to see the facts of life as they really are, however little they may be what one would like to have them; Cicero, who felt that every activity of life should be socialized and who practised what he preached, to whom the founding, development, and preservation of those assemblages of human beings which are called " States " constituted the noblest work in which a good man could engage, who gave up his life, when he was more than sixty years of age, in a heroic attempt to save the *ancien régime* which had become to him so unspeakably dear. Diverse, then, as are these three representatives of humanism, is there nevertheless a common element in the ultimate psychology of Lucretius, Horace, and Cicero? We may answer this question in the affirmative. There is such a common element, and in it is to be found the life-giving root of all the diversified efflorescence of humanism. All three men are self-reliant. All three are convinced that, while some kinds of knowledge lie beyond the ken of human reason, nevertheless this reason is fully competent in the exercise of its own native powers to discover a solution for every difficulty that imperils human happiness on this earth. They are further convinced that, since the will is free and may therefore accept or reject these discoveries of the reason, every human being can achieve a worthy ordering of his life, except in so far as he is willing to remain in bondage to ignorance and folly. Let us return for a moment to the fifteenth century and listen to Giovanni Pico della Mirandola (1463–94) whose early death at the age of thirty-one robbed the Academy of Florence and the brilliant court of Lorenzo the Magnificent and the Medici family of one of their brightest stars. Of this humanist another humanist (also a member of the Academy and even more famous), Angelo Poliziano, or Politian as he is more familiarly known to us, writes as follows:

Nature seemed to have showered on this man, or rather on this demi-god, all her gifts. He was tall and finely molded; from his face something of divinity shone forth. Acute and gifted with a prodigious memory, in his studies he was indefatigable, in his style perspicuous and eloquent. You could not say whether his talents or his moral qualities conferred on him the greater lustre. Familiar with all branches of philosophy and master of many languages, he stood on high above the reach of praise.[4]

Listen now to a passage from his *Oration on the Dignity of Man:*

Then the Supreme Maker decreed that unto Man, on whom He could bestow nought singular, should belong in common whatsoever had been given to His other creatures. Therefore He took man, made in His own individual image, and having placed him in the centre of the world, spake to him thus: " Neither a fixed abode, nor a form in thine own likeness, nor any gift peculiar to thyself alone, have we given thee, O Adam, in order that what abode, what likeness, what gifts thou shalt choose, may be thine to have and to possess. The nature allotted to all other creatures, within laws appointed by ourselves, restrains them. Thou, restrained by no narrow bounds, according to thy own free will, in whose power I have placed thee, shalt define thy nature for thyself. I have set thee midmost the world, that thence thou mightest the more conveniently survey whatsoever is in the world. Nor have we made thee either heavenly or earthly, mortal or immortal, to the end that thou, be-

[4] Quoted by John Addington Symonds in " The Revival of Learning," in *The Renaissance in Italy* (The Modern Library, 1935), I, 480.

ing, as it were, thy own free maker and molder, shouldst fashion thyself in what form may like thee best. Thou shalt have power to decline unto the lower or brute creatures. Thou shalt have power to be reborn unto the higher, or divine, according to the sentence of thy intellect." Thus to Man, at his birth, the Father gave seeds of all variety and germs of every form of life.[5]

Let me put beside this Renaissance declaration of man's competence for self-determination a passage from the essay of John Stuart Mill on " Nature," to which I have already referred.

The only admissible moral theory of Creation is that the Principle of Good *cannot* at once and altogether subdue the powers of evil, either physical or moral; could not place mankind in a world free from the necessity of an incessant struggle with the maleficent powers, or make them always victorious in that struggle, but could and did make them capable of carrying on the fight with vigour and with progressively increasing success.

In both these passages, the one a product of the Renaissance, the other of the Victorian era, we breathe the same atmosphere, and are aware of a basic faith in the resourceful and indomitable mind of man. However abundant the evidence, however apparently complete and coercive the proof that, as the exponents of the mechanistic theory so confidently assert today, man is simply a product of physical and chemical elements, a natural being in the same sense as animals, plants, and atoms, we must still note, as of old, that he is obviously the superior and the judge of the forces which have evolved him. Even if this theory be true, it is not from his antecedents and environment that he draws his standards of perfection but rather from the aspirations of his own nature. He has always had visions of a world in which his environment would be as practically helpful in enabling

[5] *Ibid.*, p. 352. For the original Latin see Pico's *Opera omnia* (Basileae, 1572–73), I, 314.

him to realize his noblest thoughts as the conditions with which an experienced gardener surrounds an orchid that will, he hopes, capture a gold medal in a competitive exhibition. He has dreamed of a cosmos in which, here and now, the wicked would not flourish " like a green bay tree," [6] but in which, instead, the reasonable happiness which humanity craves would be integrally dependent upon right action, and would follow such action as naturally and inevitably as in the physical realm matter obeys the laws of gravitation. But in the workings of nature there is discernible no sense of justice, much less any active coöperation with man's striving after righteousness. With these ideals and the like, nature has no conscious sympathy. As William James has well said:

> All that we know of good and duty proceeds from nature; but none the less so all that we know of evil. Visible nature is all plasticity and indifference, — a moral multiverse as one might call it, and not a moral universe. . . . With her as a whole we can establish no moral communion; and we are free in our dealings with her several parts to obey or destroy, and to follow no law but that of prudence in coming to terms with such of her particular features as will help us to our private ends.[7]

In the great chorus of the *Antigone* in praise of man, Sophocles says of him that " he has resource for everything; without resource he meets nothing that must come."

$$\pi \alpha \nu \tau o \pi \acute{o} \rho o \varsigma \cdot \ \ \ddot{\alpha} \pi o \rho o \varsigma \ \acute{\epsilon} \pi ' \ o \dot{v} \delta \grave{\epsilon} \nu \ \ \ddot{\epsilon} \rho \chi \epsilon \tau \alpha \iota$$
$$\tau \grave{o} \ \mu \acute{\epsilon} \lambda \lambda o \nu .^{8}$$

In the same exalted mood Lucretius, at the end of Book V of *De Rerum Natura*,[9] closes his brilliant account of

---

[6] Psalms xxxvii. 35.

[7] " Is Life Worth Living? " in *The Will to Believe and Other Essays in Popular Philosophy* (Longmans, Green & Co., 1917), pp. 43, 44.

[8] *Antigone*, 360–61.   [9] 1448–57.

the development of human society and the arts of life from the time when primitive man knew neither clothing nor fire, lived on acorns and arbute berries, and fought for his existence against beasts not much more savage than he was himself to the full efflorescence of Mediterranean civilization as Lucretius saw it:

Ships, and the tilling of the soil, city-walls, laws, weapons, roads, garments and all other things of this kind, all the prizes and luxuries of life without exception, poetry, painting, and the perfecting of masterpieces of sculpture, practice and together with this practice the experimental work of the tireless mind taught them little by little, as they went forward step by step. Thus, little by little, time brings out each separate thing into view, and reason lifts it into the precincts of light. For they saw one thing after another become clear through the use of their intellects, until they reached the heights of artistic achievement.

Navigia atque agri culturas moenia leges
arma vias vestes et cetera de genere horum,
praemia, delicias quoque vitae funditus omnes,
carmina, picturas, et daedala signa polire,
usus et impigrae simul experientia mentis
paulatim docuit pedetemptim progredientes.
Sic unum quicquid paulatim protrahit aetas
in medium ratioque in luminis erigit oras.
Namque alid ex alio clarescere corde videbant,
artibus ad summum donec venere cacumen.

Let us note now one more instance — but this the most striking of all — one more instance of that which is for me the distinguishing characteristic of humanism, an unfailing self-reliance, a deep-seated conviction that man is competent through his own nature to achieve here on earth, if he shall so resolve, a noble happiness that is commensurate with the dignity of that nature. In the so-called *Meditations* of the great Stoic emperor, Marcus Aurelius, the casual notebook which reveals to us a life that has been justly called " the normal high-water mark of the unassisted virtue of man," [10] the reader will find, from time to time, entries which show that to Marcus the alternative of " gods or atoms " — of a universe ruled either by blind chance or by an intelligent Providence — was ever present and ever unsolved. But despite recurrent doubts, despite experiences that brought him almost to the verge of despair, he elected to cling to the noblest hypothesis that he knew, and, in accordance therewith, to behave " as a member of a sacred cosmos and coöperant with the ordering gods." Fundamental in this hypothesis was the belief that the dignity of man is due to his kinship with the divine; for man alone is endowed with that reasoning faculty which is the supreme attribute of Deity. But what if the carefully marshaled proofs of a providential order are, after all, inadequate. If, after all, the world is really a welter of alternate combination and dispersion of atoms? Confronted by this distressing possibility, Marcus falls back upon his unshaken reverence for that reason and will which is sovereign in each human being. In the twelfth and last book he writes : [11]

> Either fixed necessity and an inviolable order, or a merciful providence, or a random and ungoverned medley. If an inviolable necessity, why resist? If a providence, waiting to be merciful, make yourself worthy of the divine aid. If a chaos uncontrolled, be thankful that amid the wild waters you have within yourself an inner governing mind. If the waves sweep you away, let them sweep flesh, breath, and poor mortality; the mind they shall never sweep.

In an earlier entry he had already written : " If there be a god, then all is well; if all things go at random, be not thou also a part of the random." [12] In this mood, in his

[10] F. W. H. Myers, " Marcus Aurelius Antoninus," in *Essays Classical* (Macmillan & Co., 1911), p. 223.

[11] xii. 14.   [12] ix. 28.

own grave and often somber fashion he would have echoed Henley's cry:

> I am the master of my fate;
> I am the captain of my soul.

In the care-free days of long ago, when the difficulties that beset the translation of thought into action were as yet but dimly discerned, when to the ardent optimism of youth all ideals seemed capable of realization if only the will to achieve them could be kept alert and strong, in brief, when I was still an undergraduate, I found upon the title-page of John Addington Symonds' fascinating *Studies of the Greek Poets* a quotation from Goethe:

> Im Ganzen, Guten, Schönen
> Resolut zu leben.

The words took possession of me as a veritable trumpet call to thought and consonant action. I was already groping my way towards some such comprehensive formula for civilization as Professor Albert Jay Nock employs in a recent admirable article.[13] Dr. Nock declares mankind's fundamental social instincts to be five in number — the instinct of workmanship, of intellect and knowledge, of religion and morals, of beauty and poetry, of social life and manners.

> A civilized society [he says] is one which organizes a full collective expression of all these instincts, and which so regulates this expression as to permit no predominance of one or more of them at the expense of the rest; in short, one which keeps this expression in continual harmony and balance.

As I reflected again and again upon the implications of Goethe's magical words, it was especially the opening phrase that fired my imagination. To live sensitively

[13] Albert Jay Nock, " A Word to Women," *Atlantic Monthly,* Nov., 1931, p. 552.

responsive to the Good and the Beautiful — that would
be a high calling and by no means an easy one. Still, to the
eternal honor of our easily discouraged race, thousands
of human beings have left behind them the proof that
such lives have actually been lived upon this earth. But
to live *im Ganzen,* to be free from provincialism and
parochialism, to be a citizen of a world of large horizons
and broad sympathies, to understand and use the many-
sided experience of the past to enrich the present and pre-
pare the way for an ever nobler future for all sorts and
conditions of men; not to be one, for example, of whom
it could be said,

> Primroses by the river's brim
> Dicotyledons were to him,
> And they were nothing more,

not to be one whose views on religion and politics (the
two subjects about which men have most passionately
disagreed) are so narrowly and intensely held as to pre-
clude a sympathetic understanding of the strength of the
appeal to other aspiring souls of quite different or even
antagonistic political and religious credos, " to see life
steadily and see it whole," as Matthew Arnold said of
Sophocles — so to live *im Ganzen* would evidently require, unless one were most happily constituted, rigorous
self-discipline, and a sedulous and impartial cultivation
of all five of the basic instincts which Professor Nock
enumerated in the article just referred to. Let me note
parenthetically that I do not mean to imply that I, so
many years ago, anticipated Dr. Nock. He has no reason
to say of me *Pereant qui nostra ante nos dixerunt* (The
deuce take those who expressed our fine ideas before we
expressed them ourselves). My thoughts at that time
were as yet inchoate. But Goethe's words moved me

deeply and became a permanent element in my endeavor
to understand man's true position in the universe.

In those halcyon days I was twice enthralled by a
grande passion, first for Sir Walter Scott, then for George
Eliot. Both writers broadened and clarified my conception of humanism. I had come under the spell of the
Wizard of the North, as Scott has been affectionately
called, before I entered college, and my appreciation of
the essential virility and high-mindedness of his portrayal of life has increased with the passing years. It has
been said of a well-known American novelist (whose
name, since I regard the criticism as unmerited, I will
not mention) that he described human beings chiefly in
their moments of vacuity and inanity. From such an
apotheosis of the mediocre and the commonplace, with
which the fiction of our age has made us tiresomely familiar, it is a joy to turn to the vigorous characters and
commensurate adventures of Scott's men and women.
His novels express a definite philosophy, though he did
not create his heroes and heroines to make them the
exponents of a philosophical theory. If one reads his journal and letters, one finds the definite evidence of that
Stoic strain which one must, at least, surmise from the
tales themselves. Like George Eliot, from whom in many
ways he is so strikingly different, he sees in action the
chief factor which molds character. Our habitual choices
determine our lives, and these choices are entirely within
our own control. Unlike George Eliot, he paints neither
the growth nor the deterioration of character. His *dra-
matis personae,* however variously conceived, are consistent types, and meet the perplexities and hazards of
the story in accordance with the same inner motives for
action. As I observe the zest with which they live and the

composure which they exhibit in the face of possible
death, I am reminded of Sarpedon's speech to Glaucus
in the *Iliad*:

> Friend of my soul, were it true that, if we once escaped from this
> war, we should live forever without old age or death, I should not
> fight myself among the foremost nor would I send thee into the
> battle that brings men glory. But, since a thousand fates of death
> stand over us which mortal man may not flee from nor escape, let
> us go on, and either give glory to another or win it ourselves.[14]

In Scott as in Homer, courage and self-reliance are the
watchwords, not as a pose, but as the outward and visible
signs of an inward and spiritual grace.

Of George Eliot so competent a critic as the late William C. Brownell writes as follows:

> It is as a moralist that she is a real contributor to literature, that
> she is at her best, that she is of the first class, and that, among
> novelists at least, she is, if not unrivalled, at all events unsurpassed.
> No such explicit "criticism of life" as hers exists in fiction.[15]

In this last sentence Mr. Brownell prints the words
"criticism of life" within quotation marks, and is evidently thinking of Matthew Arnold's fruitful use of the
phrase. Her novels gave me an intellectual delight the
poignancy of which is still vivid in memory. But, whereas
in Scott, my first favorite, a philosophy underlies the tale
which is, however, written for its own sake, in George
Eliot "the story and the characters themselves are conceived as examples and illustrations of the moral she has
in mind from the outset, and as a part of its systematic
presentation. The moral is her first concern." These
characters, however, to me were and have been ever since
in no sense lay figures, draped in the garments of an
evolutionary system, but rather the most real flesh and

---

[14] xii. 322–28.
[15] *Victorian Prose Masters* (Chas. Scribner's Sons, 1901), p. 139.

blood human beings. In my judgment, even Daniel
Deronda is human, although, like Vergil's Aeneas, he
does come perilously close to being the incarnation of a
complex of abstract ideas. Pervasive in all her novels is
the conception of the invariable uniformity of nature's
processes, an unchanging law which reigns no less in the
moral and spiritual life of man than it does in the physical world about him. Of these inexorable and majestic
sequences of cause and effect man may, if he so chooses,
become a willing part. If he does so conform, he will grow
in grace; if he rebels, pain and sorrow will be his portion.
Her ethical teaching is thus finely humanistic. Happiness is no arbitrary reward, like a piece of cake given to a
good child. It is the fragrant blossom of right action and is
as organically the outcome of right action as is the oak of
the acorn. Lucretius, it may be said in passing, is preach-
ing the same humanistic doctrine when, in the magnificent passage which closes his Third Book, he declares
that the imaginary punishments of famous sinners in the
mythical lower world, Tantalus, Tityos, Sisyphus, and
the Danaids, are but allegories of the very real wretchedness of those who on this earth are the slaves of superstition, sexual passion, political ambition, and insatiable
desire for the luxuries of life. Everywhere George Eliot
stresses heredity, environment, and tradition as the great
influences that shape human lives. In particular — and
here she comes close to the very heart of humanism —
" it is our deeds that determine us as much as we determine our deeds." [16] Unforgettable in *Romola* is the
analysis of the successive decisions through which Tito
Melema, at the outset of the story a lad without a vicious
impulse but who loved, like a cat, the warm sunshine of

[16] *Adam Bede,* chap. xxix.

life, committed, in the end, act after act of utter baseness because he could not bring himself to endure hardship. After Tito had openly denied that Baldassarre was his foster father, George Eliot makes this comment:

> Tito was experiencing that inexorable law of human souls that we prepare ourselves for sudden deeds by the reiterated choice of good or evil that gradually determines character.[17]

Again:

> Our lives make a moral tradition for our individual selves, as the life of mankind at large makes a moral tradition for the race; and to have once acted greatly seems a reason why we should always be noble. But Tito was feeling the effect of an opposite tradition; he had now no memories of self-conquest and perfect faithfulness from which he could have a sense of falling.[18]

But high as she rates the molding power of the corporate life of the race, profoundly as she believes that the true wisdom is always social, she yet asserts for the individual the right to rely in crises upon his reasoning faculty, and under its guidance to traverse new paths and thus by differentiation to attempt the enrichment of an already great tradition. She says of Romola, stifled by her marriage tie, that upon her mind it had suddenly " flashed that the problem before her was essentially the same as that which had lain before Savonarola [this was after he had been excommunicated] — the problem where the sacredness of obedience ended and where the sacredness of rebellion began. To her, as to him, there had come one of those moments in life when the soul must dare to act on its own warrant, not only without external law to appeal to, but in the face of a law which is not unarmed with Divine lightnings — lightnings that may yet fall if the warrant has been false." [19] In all this she is impressively

---

[17] *Romola,* chap. xxiii.   [18] *Ibid.,* chap. xxxix.
[19] *Ibid.,* chap. lvi.

humanistic, and never more so than in the exquisite poem, *The Choir Invisible,* in which she glorifies the immortality of the individual in the lengthening and uplifting tradition of the race.

Professor Henry Nettleship, in an essay [20] which, though first published in 1875, remains still in my judgment one of the most notable and illuminating contributions ever made to an adequate understanding of the poem, writes in this wise in the course of the opening paragraph:

> It may happen, on the other hand, that a great work of imagination sometimes presents such difficulties in the ordinary understanding, that, although its power and beauty are instinctively recognised by succeeding generations of men, the main thoughts which have inspired it and which are the real strength of its author are not clearly grasped, and criticism, favourable or unfavourable, lingers over details with praise, blame, explanation, or apology, while it misses the great intention which lies beneath and is the foundation of the whole.

If, now, in the spirit of this comment upon the study of great works of art, we endeavor to determine those elements in the thought of Lucretius that make him still, after nearly two thousand years, a source of lofty inspiration, we shall be led, I think, to the following conclusion. First, these elements will not be found to include the specific details of his science. His atoms are not our atoms, and no physicist, however competent, can tell us what will be the constitution of the atoms of the future. It is for us a commonplace that all scientific hypotheses are provisional only, and the fixation of the ultimate secrets of nature's processes is still extremely difficult. All this material in the poem forms an exceedingly cap-

[20] " Suggestions Introductory to a Study of the Aeneid," in *Lectures and Essays on Subjects Connected with Latin Literature* (Oxford, Clarendon Press, 1885).

tivating chapter in the history of scientific speculation, but, if this were all, *De Rerum Natura* would not be immortal. The sixth book would seem to show that Lucretius had a genuine interest in science for its own sake, something which we can hardly ascribe to Epicurus, though it was characteristic of Democritus, Epicurus' predecessor in the development of the atomic theory. But even for Lucretius the real importance of the natural sciences was due to the fact that without this knowledge it would be impossible to prove that the universe was the concrete expression of invariable law, the sole exception being the freedom of the human will. For us, then, the elements of enduring power in his work are these: his hatred of superstition, which has normally, if not indeed always, been associated with cruelty; his grandiose conception of an illimitable universe, peopled by countless systems like that of which this earth forms a part, all evolved out of unchangeable and indestructible ultimate particles of matter, all exhibiting an invariable sequence of cause and effect, so that everything, the human soul included, is what it is in virtue of its atomic constitution, in a word, an intelligible and law-abiding universe, free from any conceivable intervention of capricious anthropomorphic deities; his triumphant conviction that the human reason is in itself fully competent through observation, analysis, and interpretation of data abundantly available on every side — *species ratioque naturae* — to solve in the end every problem that imperils human happiness here on earth, in other words, his scientific temper; his equally triumphant conviction that the will is free, and that man is therefore able by his own deliberate choice so to utilize his knowledge of nature's laws " that nothing will hinder him from living a life worthy

of the gods " — *ut nil impediat dignam dis degere
vitam* [21]; his belief that the gods live a life of flawless
beatitude, a life such as every devout Epicurean would
fain achieve for himself here on earth, a life, therefore,
that is no mere vain dream but that has been actually
realized somewhere in the interstellar spaces, whence it
follows that if no false and injurious conception of their
nature interferes, one will be able to worship their perfection with tranquil peace of mind and be refreshed
thereby; [22] and, finally, his profound sense of the infinite
pathos of human life, his warm yet grave sympathy for
those who, though Epicurus has thrown so clear a light
upon the one safe road to happiness, cannot be persuaded
to accept his guidance, and choose rather to wander in
the darkness that envelops all but the followers of the
Master. Lucretius is an extraordinary representative of
his school. He preaches " passionless tranquillity " with
the enthusiasm and energy of a crusader, perhaps I
should rather say, of a missionary to the heathen. Sta-
tius speaks of his *furor arduus*,[23] and De Quincey, in his
essay on Keats, notes as a consideration that lends some
support to the tradition that *De Rerum Natura* was composed in lucid intervals between attacks of insanity,[24] the
fact that Lucretius rises into the empyrean of passionate
thought and feeling at the outset of the poem and never
descends at all, even at the close. W. H. Mallock in his
exquisite translation of certain parts of the poem in the

[21] iii. 322.   [22] vi. 68–78.
[23] *Silvae* ii. 7. 77.
[24] In his presidential address to the British Classical Association, Sir William
Osler, certainly one of the most eminent physicians of modern times, said of
Lucretius: " Of insanity of any type that leaves a mind capable in lucid intervals
of writing such verses as *De Rerum Natura* we know nothing." See Sir William
Osler, *The Old Humanities and the New Science* (Houghton, Mifflin & Co.,
1920), p. 45.

meter of Omar Khayyám, uses occasionally with entire
propriety some phrases from the Bible, such as, for
example: [25]

> Come unto me all ye that labour. Ye
> Whose souls are heavy-laden, come to me,
>   And I will lead you forth by streams that heal,
> And feed you with the truth that sets men free.

And again:

> Oh Science, lift aloud thy voice that stills
> The pulse of fear, and through the conscience thrills —
>   Thrills through the conscience with the news of peace —
> How beautiful thy feet are on the hills!

He preaches the gospel of healing death in his passionate
certainty that if only he can prove that the caprice and
anger of anthropomorphic deities (witness the sacrifice
of Iphigenia) need not be feared either in this world (for
the reign of law knows no exceptions) or in the next (for
there is no next), man, thus made unquestioned master
of his fate, can with the help of science and philosophy
order his life, without and within, in a manner that is
consonant with the dignity of his nature. He is thus a
humanist of the first rank. He lives habitually *im Ganzen,*
and gains from his generous enthusiasm for the study of
forces that operate on a grand scale in illimitable space
and in unending time a standard for the measurement of
values, as either transitory or enduring, that he employs
constantly, with all the resources of poetry to help him,
as he endeavors to present adequately and persuasively
that philosophy which insures in every recipient soul the
dethronement of illusion and the sovereignty, in its stead,
of reason.

The chapter that is devoted to Horace in Professor

[25] *Lucretius on Life and Death* (John Lane, 1900), pp. 8, 22.

Mackail's *Latin Literature* closes with the following paragraph:

Among the many amazing achievements of the Greek genius in the field of human thought were a lyrical poetry of unexampled beauty, a refined critical faculty, and later than the greater thinkers and outside of the strict schools, a temperate philosophy of life such as we see afterwards in the beautiful personality of Plutarch. In all these three Horace interpreted Greece to the world, while adding that peculiarly Roman urbanity — the spirit at once of the grown man as distinguished from children, of the man of the world, and of the gentleman — which up till now has been the dominant ideal over the thought and life of Europe.

If these statements are valid, as they certainly are, we shall not be surprised to find Horace among the humanists. He styles himself an Epicurean,[26] but he is certainly very different from Lucretius. The earlier poet is perfervid; Horace distrusts enthusiasm, feeling quite sure that such partisanship will normally result in a higher or lower appraisal of things than they actually deserve. He would fain, as I have already said of him, see the facts of life as they really are, and to that end disciplines all excess of feeling. In thus educating himself he is acting in full accord with one of the strongest elements in his nature. A partisan temperament is apt to find it difficult to see merit in views quite different from those to which it has become attached. Perhaps his most salient trait is his independence of judgment, his reliance upon his own reflections both in defining the ideal ends which an intelligent being should keep in view for the guidance of life, and in determining the nature and extent of the adjustments which must be made in the admittedly difficult process of translating thought into action. In these respects he reveals himself a true humanist. It is interest-

[26] *Epp.* i. 4. 16.

ing to observe in him the sobering effect of experience.
The enthusiasm with which in his student days at Athens
he espoused the cause of the *Liberatores* reminds us of
Wordsworth's famous lines:

> Bliss was it in that dawn to be alive;
> But to be young was very heaven.

The presence of this idealistic temper may be felt in
the sixteenth Epode in which, after the disaster at
Philippi, he calls upon those who still are loyal to the
Republic to follow him to the mythical Islands of the
Blest. But Horace had in a high degree that intelligence
which Professor Santayana declares to be " quickness in
seeing things as they are." [27] He presently became convinced that one must not expect too much of life, the
activity of Fortuna is too widespread and too incalculable; and therefore true wisdom, which in reality is common sense, enjoins the pursuit of a kind of happiness that
in a world always potentially hostile may be realized and
kept intact whether Fortuna smiles or frowns. One is
master of fate only if one is captain of one's soul. The resultant temper of mind finds expression in some of
Horace's most familiar phrases, such as, for example,
nil admirari and *aurea mediocritas* and the striking lines:

> Sed satis est orare Iovem, qui ponit et aufert,
> det vitam, det opes; aequum mi animum ipse parabo! [28]

But this *aequanimitas,* this even poise of mind, is for
Horace no Epicurean " passionless tranquillity." He
lived in one of the most beautiful countries in the world,
where nature is lavish in the display of her varied charms.
He was admitted to full rights of membership in the
highly cultivated society of the capital. His enjoyment,

[27] *Three Philosophical Poets* (Harvard University Press, 1910), p. 20.
[28] *Epp.* i. 18. 111, 112.

both of picturesque nature and of social intercourse, was keen. But if one's motto under these conditions is *carpe diem*, the question " How may one thoroughly enjoy life and yet be always serene? " resolves itself into " How may one thoroughly enjoy life and yet be independent of it? " As Horace mused over the possible solutions of this eminently practical problem he seems to have been especially drawn to Aristippus by the latter's flexibility and sunny cheerfulness in the face of untoward circumstances, his ability to be master of things, not mastered by them.[29]

In Aristippus certainly, whose attitude toward life, as tradition portrayed it, so took Horace's fancy, this philosophy of sunshine, of " sweetness " (for this is the real meaning of " hedonism ") was something more than the expression of a self-indulgent gratification of the desire for pleasure. There were in that age, as indeed there have been in every age, human beings endowed with so little strength of character that in them acceptance of the Cyrenaic tenets led to lives altogether unlovely. But for Aristippus this cult of the passing hour, this capture of the fleeting joy of the present moment, could not be successfully pursued without a certain thoughtful discipline and refinement of all the faculties of outward and inward vision. Clarity of intelligence was indispensable, and no less precision of good taste. In this process of self-education constant analysis of the phenomena alike of nature and of man would serve as an instrument of culture to the end that life itself might become the finest of all the fine arts, and find fitting expression in the gracious amenities of social intercourse. Even if one admits, as indeed one must, that this program represented rather an

[29] *Epp.* i. 1. 18, 19 and i. 17, 23, 24.

aspiration, a counsel of perfection, than a well-attested feasible ordering of daily life, if one adds, as again one must, that the translation of idealistic thought into practical action is in every walk of life beset with difficulties, one can still readily see how the measure of success attained by Aristippus made this citizen of beautiful and luxurious Cyrene an engaging figure to Horace.

The quest of this capacity to enjoy the passing moment without being in the least degree absorbed by it greatly strengthened in Horace the innate tendency to study human behavior, to speculate about the motives which prompt speech and action. In endeavoring to understand other men he is forced to depend upon inference — a somewhat unreliable instrument. In studying himself he can, in the end, be sure of the facts and their significance. He is, therefore, an inveterate analyst of the merits and defects of his own character, and has much to say about himself. But one may apply to him the words which Sidney Colvin uses of Robert Louis Stevenson in his introduction to the latter's *Vailima Letters:*

> Stevenson belonged to the race of Montaigne and the literary egotists. The word seems out of place, since of egotism in the sense of vanity or selfishness he was of all men the most devoid; but he was nevertheless a watchful and ever interested observer of the motions of his own mind. He saw himself, as he saw everything (to borrow the words of Mr. Andrew Lang), with the lucidity of genius and loved to put himself on terms of confidence with his readers.

He loves to give his friends and readers good advice. But his words and tone are so tactfully chosen as to be entirely devoid of any suggestion of superiority. Professor Rand says of St. Jerome: " He liked to go around doing good to those who did not like to be done good to." [30] In

[30] *Founders of the Middle Ages,* (Harvard University Press, 1928), p. 105.

this respect Horace would have found St. Jerome somewhat "impossible." Whistler wrote a famous book entitled *The Gentle Art of Making Enemies.* We sadly need
for our political and social life a textbook upon the gentle
art of becoming and remaining helpful friends of those
with whose views and resultant behavior we cannot ourselves at the moment agree. What I have now to say
about the ways in which Horace may help us in these days
has no doubt already suggested itself to many Horatians
here present. For no characteristic of Horace's personality as revealed in his writings, especially as years
brought him the philosophic mind, is more striking than
the value which he attaches to social tact. In all the intercourse of life he was scrupulously observant of the
likes and dislikes of his associates, ever concerned to be
dulcis amicis, and especially so when he had occasion to
present some different view which implied a criticism.
You will recall how in writing to Celsus Albinovanus he
takes special pains to dwell upon his own imperfections
before he ventures to suggest a certain change of conduct
to Celsus.[31] He was always, it would appear, fully aware
how perilous a thing it is to give advice, how reasonable
is the preference of mankind for its own way, and yet how
often success may be won by careful choice of phrase,
tone, and manner. Certainly nothing could be more
charming than the letter in which he suggests to Maecenas that the latter's friendship and innumerable kind-
nesses to him cannot, and of course will not, be allowed to deprive him of his liberty.[32] Recall too the letter
in which he introduces Septimius to Tiberius, and note
the grace with which, in explaining why he has sent it, he
disclaims the right to intrude his wishes upon the young

[31] *Epp.* i. 8.   [32] *Ibid.,* i. 7.

prince.[33] Suspicious as Tiberius may have been, he could not have felt as he read this letter that it trenched in the slightest degree upon his right to choose his associates for himself. Perhaps the most striking and most definite expression of his kindliness in judging his friends is to be found in the third Satire of the first Book where he suggests the terms that should be used in describing friends whose characteristics lay them open in one way or another to criticism:

> Parcius hic vivit: frugi dicatur. Ineptus
> et iactantior hic paulo est: concinnus amicis
> postulat ut videatur. At est truculentior atque
> plus aequo liber: simplex fortisque habeatur.
> Caldior est: acres inter numeretur. Opinor,
> haec res et iungit iunctos et servat amicos.[34]

Everywhere we find in Horace that exquisite urbanity which is the outward and visible sign of an inward deference to the right of others to be themselves and to work out with his kindly help their own salvation. He claims for himself the privilege of being independent and claims it no less for others. Is he himself a *sapiens* in a world of *stulti?* He has far too keen a sense of humor to believe this, and his writings are full of passages in which he is apparently as much amused at his own oddities as at those of others. In two Satires of the second Book, the third and the seventh, Horace turns the laugh against himself, Damasippus in the first case and Davus in the second being made to discuss Horace's own shortcomings in order to attack indirectly the failings of men in general. I need not point out to you how potent a factor in making and keeping friends is such entire freedom from undue self-esteem. That independence which he

<hr>

[33] *Ibid.,* i. 9.   [34] *Sat.* i. 3. 49–54.

claims for himself he was scrupulously careful to accord to others, and in taking this position he was actuated not so much by any feeling of personal conscience as by a recognition of the value of such an attitude in furthering the ends for which human intercourse deserves to exist.

The studied avoidance of any suggestion of superior excellence was in Horace no dramatic pose. No poet is more conscious of his limitations. He is sincerely anxious not to have others regard him as better than he knows himself to be. He finds in himself a representative human being, not too wise or good for human nature's daily food of praise and blame. His shafts of genial irony are aimed no less frequently at himself than at those about him. Yet at heart he is profoundly serious. His mature work, especially the patriotic Odes, afford ample evidence of his genuine and unfailing interest in the grave social problems of his time. Nevertheless, in dealing with this world he felt, as Gratiano says to Antonio in *The Merchant of Venice,*

> They lose it that do buy it with much care.

It is possible to be so serious-minded that with the best of intentions one may do actual harm. In the tale entitled " A Germ Destroyer " Kipling describes an amusing situation of this general type. But there are grave cases also, as he shows in another tale entitled " Thrown Away." A sense of humor is thus indispensable for the constructive development of human intercourse. But this humor must be sympathetic rather than scornful. For, as Carlyle says in his essay on Richter, " true humor is sensibility in the most catholic and deepest sense." The constant play in Horace of such a sense of humor is one of his most engaging characteristics.

In the development of the argument of *Paradise Lost*
Milton tells us how Raphael was sent to warn Adam of
impending danger to his happiness; and how the Archangel, after relating the story of Satan's revolt, the war
in heaven, and the final expulsion of the rebellious angels,
describes the creation of the new world. His eloquence
leads Adam to express some wonder that so dazzling a
sidereal universe was apparently created merely to give
light and warmth to the relatively insignificant earth.
Raphael, in reply, without taking sides in the astronomi-
cal dispute, gives a glowing exposition of both the Ptolemaic and the Copernican explanations of the motions of
the heavenly bodies, and gravely advises his hearer not
to let his thoughts dwell on matters that were intention-
ally wrapped in mystery. Adam at once agrees, declaring

> That not to know at large of things remote
> From use, obscure and subtle, but to know
> That which before us lies in daily life,
> Is the prime wisdom.[35]

In this declaration we breathe at once the atmosphere of
humanism; we are at once concerned with the problem
how to realize and safeguard here and now a happiness
commensurate with the dignity of man's nature. And in
regard to the other necessary element in humanism, as I
have essayed above to define it, the Renaissance ideal of
the independence of the individual, the development of
personal power in manifold ways, let us remember that,
as the late George E. Woodberry says in his fine appreciation of Milton,

the key to Milton's intellectual life lies in his Renaissance training;
personal force, such as he raised to heroic proportions in Satan, was
his ideal, personal liberty civil and religious, in all its forms, was the

[35] viii. 191–94.

thing nearest to his heart. He was true Puritan, full grown, not in the sense of the sectaries of his age but in that which is for all time, the man free from all forms who needs no intermediary with his God except the spiritual Christ.[36]

Wordsworth wrote of him: " Thy soul was like a star and dwelt apart." But Milton was none the less a practical idealist, absorbed, especially during the middle period of his life, in the endeavor, through the medium of a lofty and impassioned prose, to make ideal principles operative in the life of his country. He thundered against the Stuart line as Cicero did against Antony. Both men were stanch defenders of personal liberty against the encroachments of tyranny.

If, now, we consider again Adam's reply to Raphael and take it in connection with its context, we shall find implicit in it an important philosophical attitude of mind. The spiritual meaning of the universe remains for us unimpaired even if we do not understand or even care to know all the precise details of its constitution and behavior. The Ptolemaic cosmogony which Milton uses is a grandiose conception. There is in the Greek Anthology an epigram in which Ptolemy himself expresses his ecstasy as he works at his favorite science: [37]

I know that I am mortal and ephemeral; but when I scan the multitudinous circling spirals of the stars, no longer do I touch earth with my feet, but sit with Zeus himself and take my fill of the ambrosial food of gods.

Οἶδ' ὅτι θνατὸς ἐγὼ καὶ ἐφάμερος· ἀλλ' ὅταν ἄστρων
μαστεύω πυκινὰς ἀμφιδρόμους ἕλικας
οὐκέτ' ἐπιψαύω γαίης ποσίν, ἀλλὰ παρ' αὐτῷ
Ζανὶ θεοτρεφέος πίμπλαμαι ἀμβροσίης.

[36] " Milton," in *Great Writers*, pp. 90, 91.
[37] J. W. Mackail, *Select Epigrams from the Greek Anthology* (Longmans, Green & Co., 1906), p. 175.

If, in harmony with Goethe's words, quoted above, we are resolved to live not only in the Good and the Beautiful (all lovers of the Beautiful do not live in the Good; witness Robert Browning's " My Last Duchess ") but also in the Whole, we shall need a philosophy which embraces all that is. If, further, we are humanists, we shall work out such a philosophy for ourselves, and we shall not be satisfied unless it furthers the realization from day to day of a life of noble and intelligent thought, feeling, and action. The problem is eminently practical, not theoretical.

> To know
> That which before us lies in daily life,
> Is the prime wisdom.

Upon the acquisition and intelligent use of this knowledge all other kinds of knowledge and understanding converge, to the end that mankind may have true life here on earth, and may have it more abundantly.

SOME PHASES OF INTELLIGENCE[1]

Intelligence is quickness in seeing things as they are.[2]

IN ONE OF Disraeli's earlier novels, *Contarini Fleming,* a study of the development of the poetic temperament, the youthful hero, romantic, imaginative, already in some measure vaguely conscious of his future, is represented as rebelling against his work at school, which seems to him to be concerned with mere words instead of with ideas. He leaves the school, appears unexpectedly before his father, at that moment on the eve of realizing his ambition to become Prime Minister of his country, and states the reason for the step which he has taken. The reply is swift and disconcerting: " Some silly book has filled your head, Contarini, with these ridiculous notions about the respective importance of words and ideas. Few ideas are correct ones, and which are correct no one can ascertain; but with words we govern men." This view of the relative importance of ideas and of the words in which different people express, sometimes thoughtfully but far more frequently without conscious thought, their personal conception of those ideas, savors of cynicism, but a dispassionate observer is forced to admit that the course of human events seems often to justify it. The power of general terms and phrases to mislead or at least to obscure comprehension, and to enable the users of them to converse with the full semblance of knowledge without, however, thinking, or knowing what those terms

---

[1] Founders' Day address at Sweet Briar College, Virginia, October 21, 1927. Reprinted from *Bulletin* of the College for Nov., 1927.

[2] George Santayana, *Three Philosophical Poets*, p. 20.

precisely mean, was noted long before Socrates immortalized the situation for the imagination of men by his persistent endeavor to discover whether his fellow citizens attached any definite and coherent notions to the general terms that they were using every day. If we could recall Socrates to life and could listen to the conversations in which, in his familiar manner, he would try to enrich his own mind by the reputed intelligence of distinguished residents of one or another city of the United States, we should almost certainly have the same sensations that we now have when we read the dialogues of Plato. As Professor John Dewey has admirably said: " What is called pure thought, thought freed from the empirical contingencies of life, would, even if it existed, be irrelevant to the guidance of action. For the latter always operates amid the circumstance of contingencies." [3] If we admit, as we all do, that words are mere symbols of ideas, mere counters for things, the real things of which life is made up, then, if we wish to think straight, we shall think, for example, of generosity, not as we usually do, in a purely general way, but always in terms of the specific attitude of mind and the specific concrete act which that word could properly be used to describe in connection with a particular situation at a particular time in a particular place. All thinking that is really clear and really valuable, all thinking that is conducive to intelligent understanding of man in his world either takes this form, or may at once, if a modern Socrates should ask for closer definition, be reduced to it. In the greatest sermon ever preached, the Sermon on the Mount, we read " Blessed are the meek, for they shall inherit the earth." If these words are anything but mere

[3] *German Philosophy and Politics* (Henry Holt & Co., 1915), p. 11.

words, then they represent specific acts at specific times in specific places. If, as I said before, we wish to think straight, we shall ask ourselves the pitiless question: To what acts here and now shall these words lead in our own personal lives, in the corporate life of our city, of our state, and of our nation? What precisely do we mean today by such phrases as " freedom of speech," " self-expression," " the right to be happy," " international obligations," " Americanism "? I am not now limiting the range of possible definitions of these and of other similar general terms. I am simply urging the necessity of attaching to them, if we use them at all, a definite and consistent idea, and the further necessity of employing them in such a way that our interlocutors cannot help understanding what we mean even if they are too indolent or too indifferent to make any particular effort to do so. Nothing is more dangerous than a half truth, because the vitality of the part that is true helps insidiously to quicken the part that is false; and the worst enemy of the spread of intelligence is not error, but nebulous thinking.

It may be said, I think, without fear of contradiction, that a prime function of all education is to inculcate and foster clarity of thought and clarity of expression. May we add with equal fearlessness, that a persistent effort to understand the world in which for a brief space we live, and to express that understanding in unequivocal terms, must necessarily form certain habits of mind, the philosophic outlook, the catholic and therefore temperate judgment, the interest in knowledge as an indispensable means for the development of a rational civilization? If with Keats we may say

> Much have I travell'd in the realms of gold
> And many goodly states and kingdoms seen,

do we remain, after all, our original provincial selves? Or do we gain a genuine enfranchisement of the soul and become citizens of a larger world? Do we form the habit of mind that Cicero in his *Brutus,* a history of Roman oratory, ascribes to the really accomplished orator: " a man," he says, " who is able to create in the minds of his hearers a lively comprehension of the general principles and universal relations that are implicit in a case whose details have apparently only a local and temporal character "? The Latin runs: *Qui dilatare possit atque a propria ac definita disputatione hominis ac temporis ad communem quaestionem universi generis orationem traducere.*[4] Do we, I say, form such a habit of mind, or have we still kinship with the English lady mentioned by Emerson in his *English Traits* who, traveling on the Rhine and hearing a German speak of her party as foreigners, exclaimed, " No, we are not foreigners; we are English; it is you that are foreigners." There is a striking passage in the essay of Francis Bacon " Of the Advancement of Learning ":

> I cannot but be raised to this persuasion, that this third period of time will far surpass that of the Greek and the Roman learning; if only men will know their own strength and their own weakness both; and take, one from the other, light of invention and not fire of contradiction; and esteem of the inquisition of truth as of an enterprise and not as of a quality or ornament.[5]

Is it perhaps true that we who are interested in education, whether as teachers or as students, regard the search for truth as a quality or ornament rather than as an enterprise? In our study of literature, history, and philosophy, do we perhaps busy ourselves simply with the achievements of Greek and Roman learning and fail

---

[4] *Brutus,* 322.   [5] " Everyman's Library," p. 208.

" to make habitually our own the natural sources from which the Greeks drew for themselves and the rational spirit which kindled their imagination " [6]? We are, *ex hypothesi,* lovers of literature. Now literature, like all the fine arts, provides us with noble pleasure; but surely we may define its supreme function to be the criticism and interpretation of life. And when we consider the Protean character of life, that infinite variety which " age cannot wither nor custom stale," we may properly, I think, amplify this definition by saying that this interpretation of man to himself must be made in such a moving and broadening fashion that his comprehension of the possibilities of his nature, of its many-sided capacities of new growth and new achievement, will make it difficult for him to be satisfied with a provincial outlook on this subject, or to rest content within fixed boundaries.

If now one studies literature in this way as the sublimated essence of the life of mankind, one cannot but gain a lively sense, on the one hand, of the essential similarity of the problems which man has attempted to solve, and on the other, of the very great difference of the solutions which have been offered. *Quot homines, tot sententiae.* Are these solutions the outcome of sincere thinking? I cannot doubt it. Are the solutions sound because, if, or when, they are the outcome of sincere thinking? In Horace's words, *renuit negitatque Sabellus.*[7] It is obvious that an affirmative answer cannot be defended. I am driven to an important conclusion: sincerity of conviction affords no guarantee whatever that a proposed course of action is sound and right; or expressed more fully, sincerity of conviction considered in

---

[6] F. J. E. Woodbridge, " The Enterprise of Learning," *Columbia University Quarterly,* XIV (1912), p. 254.   [7] *Epp.* i. 16. 49.

itself alone, and without reference to the breadth, precision, and *impersonal* character of the induction upon which it is based, is a wholly inadequate justification of any action whatever. The real justification is furnished by something quite different, viz., the *dispassionate* conclusions of an acute and far-seeing intelligence. We cannot accept as true in this connection the reply of Hamlet to Rosencrantz and Guildenstern; "There is nothing either good or bad, but thinking makes it so." Individual opinion is not the final touchstone of the truth; and, inasmuch as human society is only the aggregate of the individuals that compose it, we cannot maintain that a given belief, such as, for instance, the belief in witchcraft, in a geocentric universe, or in the protecting power of a rabbit's foot, though open to question if held by a few persons only, becomes valid and unassailable if held by a whole community, a nation, or an age. The real facts still remain the real facts, unaffected by the inveterate propensity of the great majority of mankind to clothe and disguise them in its own feelings and opinions, to view them in the colors of its own predilections and prejudices. Under the guidance of the modern scientific spirit, we are learning slowly, very slowly, to distrust the necessary and universal validity of our own personal beliefs and disbeliefs. The possibilities of our own individual minds are not, after all, coterminous with the possibilities of the truth. This discovery may be surprising and disconcerting, but it is prerequisite to fullness of understanding of the objective facts. I maintain, then, that in proportion as a man prizes intelligence above instinct and emotion, he will not so far trust even his own beliefs, much less those of others, as to perform actions the consequences of which must be disastrous unless these beliefs are

wholly sound. He will be sure that an act which, if performed by a bad man for a bad purpose, would seem to
all normal minds clearly bad, does not in any sense become a good act when it is performed by a good man
for a good purpose. Let us face the dilemma unflinch-
ingly. If, as we believe, there is a divine government of
the world, God wills or does not will, at a specific junc-
ture in human affairs, that course of action, approval
of which we in all sincerity, in passionate, even fanati-
cal sincerity, if you like, choose to impute to Him. But
it is obvious that His actual attitude is in nowise con-
tingent upon or conditioned by our perception or comprehension of it. It is an objective fact, completely
beyond our control, which, if we are religiously minded,
it is our highest joy to understand and further, our deepest distress to misconceive and therefore hinder. It matters not whether this thesis be stated in terms of religion
or of science, whether we define the object of our alle-
giance by the word *God* or by the word *Truth*. In either
case, if we are grown-up men and women and have put
away childish things, we shall regard ourselves as the
sworn servants of the facts as they really are, not of the
facts as we conceive them to be, and we shall be liter-
ally overwhelmed by the discovery, if such unhappiness shall come to us, that with a purity of motive
which an archangel might envy, we have been obstruct-
ing the success of a movement that was right, because
we misunderstood it and thought that it was wrong.
Objective facts are stubborn things. In Kipling's story
about Reingelder and the German Flag, a species of
coral snake so called because its skin is red, black, and
white, Reingelder is bitten and dies because he trusted
the assurance of a distinguished ophiologist that the

bite of a coral snake was never poisonous. His ignorance of the truth, though seemingly justified, did not
exempt him from the operation of a law of physiologi-
cal chemistry. But the sequence of cause and effect is
operative not only in the world of the natural sciences.
It is discernible also in our mental processes and in
the rational and emotional achievements of mankind
as recorded in history. Here also then we must believe
that salvation is dependent upon knowledge, and that
ignorance of the facts or of their real as opposed to their
apparent import, however natural or indeed inevitable
in view of a given man's environment, not only will
imperil his own success and happiness, but, in so far as
his dealings with his fellow men are influenced by his
sincerely held but actually erroneous conception of
these facts, will make him a menace to their success
and happiness also. Still, as of yore, the most striking
aspect of the interplay of individuals is the persistent
effort of those who would fain organize society in conformity with their own personal philosophy to mold
into their own likeness those who may be induced or
coerced to follow them. In practice the desire to achieve
results as soon as possible has led to a far greater use of
coercion, overt or subtle, than of persuasion. Such a trend
toward assimilation is perhaps an inevitable outcome of
human nature. I am not thinking of the rôle that selfish-
ness has played in marring or making the lives of others;
the motives have often been of the purest, the aims of the
noblest. But able and vigorous minds do not readily
grant admission even to a suspicion, much less to a real
doubt, that policies to them so clearly sound, so abundantly justified by their own thought and experience,
may yet fail to produce happiness for personalities quite

differently constituted from themselves. If to this confidence in the accuracy of their own intellectual processes there be added the liking to control, a feeling so native to humanity that it may reasonably dispute with the desire for fame the honor of being called, in Milton's phrase, " the last infirmity of noble mind," what wonder that to men thus endowed the propriety of a nice attention to the peculiar likes and dislikes, beliefs and disbeliefs, hopes and fears, of their fellow beings has seemed an amiable but idle fancy. But as Dean Swift long ago reminded us: " There is none so blind as he who will not see." To comprehend sympathetically the many-sidedness of human life is a rare faculty; it is a plant of slow growth, and to grow at all needs constant care. Only determined and rigorous self-discipline will enable one more and more to understand the reasons for the appeal to others of ideas with which one cannot oneself agree. Unless, however, we are so egotistic and so comfortably childish as to be always sure that we are quite right, the lack of this comprehension will often, perhaps lamentably often, hide from us objective facts of great significance and beauty. You will recall possibly Hawthorne's description in his romance of *The Marble Faun* of the journey taken by Kenyon and Donatello from Monte Beni to Perugia. The route of the two friends took them now through the smiling countryside, now through ancient hill-towns, and in these latter they were especially drawn to the churches and moved by the glory of the medieval windows. On one such occasion, after spending some time within the edifice, then flooded with the bright Italian sunshine,

the friends left the church, and as they looked up from the exterior, at the window which they had just been contemplating within, nothing was visible but the merest outline of dusky shapes. Neither the individual likeness of saint, angel, nor Saviour, and far less the combined scheme and purport of the picture, could anywise be made out. That miracle of radiant art, thus viewed, was nothing better than an incomprehensible obscurity, without a gleam of beauty to induce the beholder to attempt unraveling it.

"All this," thought the sculptor, "is a most forcible emblem of the different aspects of religious truth and sacred story, as viewed from the warm interior of belief or from its cold and dreary outside. Christian faith is a grand cathedral, with divinely pictured windows. Standing without, you see no glory, nor can possibly imagine any; standing within, every ray of light reveals a harmony of unspeakable splendors."

In this passage Kenyon speaks as a believer in Christianity; but a believer in any other of the historic faiths might express his feeling in similar language. William James wrote a remarkable book on the *Varieties of Religious Experience;* the masterpieces of the world's literature place in our hands scores of remarkable books on the *Varieties of Social Experience,* imaginative portrayals of the inner life of man in connection with the problems of nature and of human society that continually imperil his happiness. There is as yet no warrant in history for believing that the subtle essence which we call personality will ever become standardized in the race as a whole. However completely the facts of nature, in all the possible senses of that highly ambiguous word, shall become scientifically known, different personalities will attach to these facts a varying significance and thus obtain different answers to the same problem. This inherently Protean character of the human mind is itself an objective fact, no less significant for the statesman in the field of politics and government than are the properties of matter for the physician in the field of physiology and hygiene. If I offer to my guests at dinner poisonous mushrooms, neither they nor I will be saved from death by the plea that I honestly believed, and indeed was apparently justified in believing, that these mushrooms were not poisonous. If we live, as science has now compelled us to believe, in an ordered universe of law, it is always the objective fact that counts in the sequence of cause and effect. In like manner, in that broad field which is somewhat vaguely described and designated by the word " sociology," effect follows cause no less surely, though the mode of operation of these laws is as yet not always clear even to experts. Here then, as elsewhere, however positive a man may be that his views and his resultant policy are sound, they may yet in the issue be found to be unsound. It follows that whenever, as Caesar in his *Commentaries on the Gallic War* acutely observes, decisions are made, *quod fere libenter homines id quod volunt credunt*,[8] " because human beings are predisposed to believe in the truth of that which they ardently desire to be true," these decisions are, precisely to that extent, the expression of a lack of intelligence. For " Nature is her own standard; and if she seems to us unnatural, there is no hope for our minds." [9] As Vergil said:

Felix qui potuit rerum cognoscere causas.[10]
Happy he who hath availed to know the causes of things.

Happy indeed! for science, which is the concrete proof of the existence of intelligence, is not merely a slowly increasing body of knowledge. It is the fruit of something even more important, a habit of the mind. As Dean Woodbridge of Columbia has finely said: " It is the

[8] iii. 18. He makes a similar remark in his *Commentaries on the Civil War: nam quae volumus et credimus libenter, et quae sentimus ipsi, reliquos sentire speramus.* ii. 27.

[9] George Santayana, *Three Philosophical Poets*, p. 28.

[10] *Georgics* ii. 490.

habit of recognizing that there is a reasonable way of doing things as over against a passionate, impulsive, instinctive, or partisan way of doing things, and that this way is discoverable through inquiry." [11] Huxley in a striking passage declared that " education is the instruction of the intellect in the laws of nature," " under which I include," he says, " not merely things and their forces but men and their ways, and the fashioning of the affection and the will into an earnest and loving desire to move in harmony with their laws." [12] Matthew Arnold, who was, as you know, by no means usually in agreement with Huxley, takes essentially the same position when he defines the end of culture to be, in the words of Bishop Wilson, " to make reason and the will of God prevail." [13] But it is obvious that before we can make the will of God prevail, we must first find out what is the will of God. We cannot hope to succeed if we substitute for that objective and unalterable fact our own crude conceptions of it. We must, therefore, discipline our desires and emotions, our instincts and impulses, by bringing them under the control of progressive intelligence.

Where may we go to become inspired with a passion for intelligence? Let me quote to you a fine passage from the opening chapter of Professor Butcher's discussion of *Some Aspects of the Greek Genius.*

The Greeks before any other people of antiquity, possessed the love of knowledge for its own sake. To see things as they really are, to discern their meaning and adjust their relations, was with them an instinct and a passion. Their methods in science and philosophy might be very faulty, and their conclusions often ab-

[11] " The Importance of Philosophy," *Columbia University Quarterly,* Sept., 1917, p. 382.
[12] " A Liberal Education," in *Lectures and Lay Sermons,* " Everyman's Library," pp. 58, 59.
[13] *Culture and Anarchy,* chap. i.

surd, but they had that fearlessness of intellect which is the first condition of seeing truly. Poets and philosophers alike looked with unflinching eye on all that met them, on man and the world, on life and death. They interrogated Nature, and sought to wrest her secret from her, without misgiving and without afterthought. Greece, first smitten with the passion for truth, had the courage to put faith in reason, and in following its guidance to take no count of consequences. "Those," says Aristotle, "who would rightly judge the truth must be arbitrators and not litigants." [14] "Let us follow the argument whithersoever it leads" [15] may be taken not only as a motto of the Platonic philosophy, but as expressing one side of the Greek genius.

Let me add a noble passage from the *Ethics* of Aristotle, whom Dante, you will remember, calls *il maestro di color che sanno*,[16] " the master of those who know ":

If reason is divine in comparison with human nature, then the life of reason is divine in comparison with human life. They are not right who say that men should think of human things and mortals of mortal things. For a man should, as far as in him lies, aim at immortality and do everything with a view to living in the light of the highest that is in him. For although that is small in size, in power and honor it far excels all the rest.[17]

If we study Greek literature aright, we shall mount to the sources that inspired it. We shall be led to the formation of a habit of mind indispensable in business, in the professions, in government, in a word, in all civilized human intercourse. For no advance in civilization, no advance in cultivation, is possible except in so far as the minds of men can be brought to enjoy the constant companionship of ideas and to prefer the guidance of reason to that of personal likes and dislikes. We shall gain from Greece her most precious gift, an ardent belief in the sovereign power of intelligence. We shall learn to follow the argument fearlessly, whithersoever it leads us, if the

[14] *De caelo* i. 10.
[15] *Laws* ii. 667 A; *Republic* iii. 394 D.
[16] *Inferno*, Canto iv. 131.
[17] 1177 E.

evidence adduced is adequate, and not to follow it, however confirmatory it may be of our personal hopes, unless we are sure that it is objectively valid, in the precise sense in which salt is unalterably salt, and never sugar or pepper. For from our contact with the Greek spirit we shall learn, though with difficulty and many a failure, to judge as arbitrators, not as litigants, knowing full well that in the words of a great English scientist, Professor J. Arthur Thomson,

our interpretations are necessarily colored by our personal experience and our social environment, our hypotheses may arise from social suggestions, but before they pass into the framework of science they must be "depersonalized"; that, in fact, the validity of a scientific conclusion, as distinguished from a mere opinion, depends upon the elimination of the subjective element.[18]

At this point you will perhaps raise a question. Man, you will say, is a social and political animal, not a solitary. Granted that the free play of the spirit of inquiry has been the greatest, if not the sole, cause of progress, has it not in the course of history been highly dangerous to the stability of nations? The bases of society have been instinct and custom. Is it not true that intellectual inquiry by weakening these bases has often led to disintegration? It must be frankly admitted that the general tendency of the intellectual life is centrifugal and that this tendency away from community modes of thought is apt to be noticeable in direct proportion to the vigor of personality and strength of intellect possessed by those who think. Greece through all her history never exhibited in any one of her various states the cohesive power that is demanded by the life of a modern nation. Rome, on the contrary, whose quick responsiveness to ideals and whose

[18] *Introduction to Science* (Henry Holt and Company, 1911), p. 25.

intellectual creative power are not to be compared with those of Greece, developed a government that gathered under its sway all the countries of the Mediterranean basin and not a few beyond, and presented for more than a thousand years an organic political growth. The Roman mind, like the British, had a sane distrust of proposals that were supported by considerations chiefly theoretical. It was instinctively aware of the difference between the world of thought and the world of action. This difference was for the Roman, as it is still for us, of prime importance. If we consider the world of thought by itself, we must, in so far as we are believers in the value of rationality, emphasize to the utmost the desirability of quick responsiveness to ideas. The intellectual life cannot possibly be too varied nor the swiftness of our recognition of the significance of new facts and ideas too great. In this world we are ever learning, ever openminded, ever in a condition of unstable equilibrium. We may, and indeed must, if the evidence is adequate, change our opinions every day. We must say with Cicero: *modo hoc, modo illud probabilius.*[19] And so long as we stay within the confines of thought and discussion alone, no unfortunate consequences will follow even from kaleidoscopic change. But the instant thought takes shape in action, we are forced to take account of the consequences of our decision. If one is about to erect a skyscraper, one must consider carefully the details of the foundation. Once laid, the foundation excludes certain possibilities that were theoretically present before. It is no longer possible to change one's mind conveniently every day, or even every month. In fact, ridiculous as it may seem at first sight, if the change contemplated in-

[19] *Academica* ii. 121.

volves a substantial or actual reversal of policy, it is less inconvenient to change one's mind every day than every month, for it is obvious that the longer the period of time during which one is executing one's plans, the more numerous become the resultant new obligations and the greater the consequent difficulty of effecting a rapid series of changes. In the world of action conservatism of some sort is a necessity and a certain slowness of responsiveness to ideas often an asset to a statesman, to a people, to an individual. But to discover the distinction between the two worlds of thought and action, to learn that conclusions reached in the first are not necessarily valid at once for the second, to remember always that action takes place not in an ideal world but among human beings as yet in myriad diverse ways imperfect — all this is in a high degree the work of intelligence. Communities and nations cannot otherwise be permanently organized. No wonder, then, that Ennius, writing when Rome had been in existence over five hundred and fifty years, could say with fervor

Moribus antiquis res stat Romana virisque.

Upon her ancient ways and men standeth the Roman State.

No wonder that Rome, endowed with strong desire to realize in human life a practicable order, should have placed a high value upon precedent, and become great for all time through her mastery of the principles and the application of law.

If the foregoing analysis is sound, we who believe in the permanent value of these monuments of human thought that have stood the test of time have, ready to our hand, implicit in rich abundance in the material that the centuries have accumulated, two of the most potent concepts for real education in the art of living that have ever come

to the human mind, the concept, on the one hand, of un-
limited freedom of inquiry in the world of investigation
and reflection, quite isolated from any consideration of
possible resultant action in human society; on the other
hand, the concept of the inestimable value of an orderly advance in the better organization of this human
society,

> Where Freedom slowly broadens down
> From precedent to precedent.

Here, if permanence be desired, the advance, as Tennyson said, must needs be slow; for, however easy it may
be to define freedom in the ideal world of thought, the
attempt still, as always, bristles with difficulties when
made in our actual world of imperfect human beings.

If these two concepts are really great and germinative,
how may we make them effective in early and in adult
education? Can we hope to teach these concepts as we
can impart to others, young and old, the facts, historically
and logically concatenated, that form the magnificent
structure of the liberal arts and sciences? Such a hope, in
my judgment, is quite illusory. Knowledge of this kind
is too mechanically conceived by the recipient mind to
have any noticeable effect upon spontaneous thinking
and spontaneous action. But if we ourselves incarnate
these ideas, if these ideas, in their various phases, pervade
our behavior as students and teachers in that school of
experience which begins in the cradle and closes only
with death, pervade our behavior as sunlight and air fill
space, we shall call into action the most powerful social
force in the world, the winning power of personality. It
is only through this vague, but almost magical influence
of personality that we can hope to kindle in other minds
that passion for intelligence, alike in its theoretical and

in its practical aspects, of which I have been speaking. To intelligence we ourselves owe all our scholarship, to intelligence, alert and uncompromising in its persistent search for the truth as it really is, the objective fact as it is, was, and ever shall be, without any regard whatever to our personal likes and dislikes, however strong these may be. Consider — for nothing is more pertinent to the needs of our daily thought and feeling if we prize intelligence — consider the picture which anthropology has gradually been able to draw for us of the history of mankind from those far-distant ages when as yet man had neither language nor fire down to the wonders of our own times. The pageant of man in history, his slow advance (incredibly slow at first) during the thousands and thousands of years that preceded the dawn of historic civilization, followed by the wonderful efflorescence and kaleidoscopic change of his life in the Orient, in Egypt, in Greece, and in the far-flung dominion of Rome — this pageant presents to us a series of events of the most diversified character in which the principle of metamorphosis is continually at work. Let us add now in our imagination the changes in society and government, in the arts of life, and in ideas and ideals in every field of thought that have marked medieval and modern history. Are we not forced to admit that change is the hallmark of life? But if this be true, if change is really the universal law, we must, if we desire to be intelligent beings, welcome its entrance into our intellectual and spiritual life. We must address ourselves to the problem of an ever-changing world with minds ever open to new aspects of truth already discovered and the transforming power of new truths never known before. In one of his finest stories Hans Christian Andersen has genially satirized the attitude of mind that is hopeless. You will recall that in his account of " The Ugly Duckling " the unfortunate creature came presently to a peasant's hut where lived a woman with her tomcat and her hen.

The Tom Cat was master of the house, and the Hen was the lady, and always said "We and the world," for she thought that they were half the world and by far the better half. The Duckling thought one might have a different opinion, but the Hen would not allow it. " Can you lay eggs? " she asked. " No." " Then you will have the goodness to hold your tongue." And the Tom Cat said " Can you curve your back and purr and give out sparks? " " No." " Then you cannot have any opinion of your own when sensible people are speaking."

The Duckling sat in a corner and was melancholy. Then the fresh air and sunshine streamed in, and it was seized with such a strange longing to swim on the water that it could not help telling the Hen of it. " What are you thinking of? " cried the Hen. " You have nothing to do. That is why you have these fancies. Purr, or lay eggs, and they will soon pass over." " But it is so charming to swim on the water," said the Duck, " so refreshing to let it close above one's head, and to dive down to the bottom." " Yes, that must be a mighty pleasure truly," quoth the Hen. " I fancy you must have gone crazy. Ask the Cat about it — he is the cleverest animal I know — ask him if he likes to swim on the water or to dive down; I won't speak about myself. Ask our mistress, the old woman; no one in the world is cleverer than she. Do you think she has any desire to swim and let the water close above her head? "

" You don't understand me," said the Duckling. " We don't understand you? Then, pray, who is to understand you? You surely don't pretend to be cleverer than the Tom Cat and the old woman — I won't say anything about myself. Don't be conceited, child, and be grateful for all the kindness you have received. Did you not get into a warm room, and have you not fallen into company from which you may learn something? But you are a chatterer and it is not pleasant to associate with you. You may believe me, I speak for your good. I tell you disagreeable things, and by that one may always know one's true friends. Only take care that you learn to lay eggs, or to purr and give out sparks." " I think I will go out into the wide world," said the Duckling. " Yes, do go," replied the Hen. And the Duckling went.

Let us cheerfully admit that not all Ugly Ducklings turn out to be swans. Let us admit also that human experience justifies not infrequently the philosophy of the Tom Cat and the Hen. Even so, the genially phrased indictment is valid and convincing. The world is still full of earnest men and women who entertain no doubt of the correctness of their own views of life, and who never even suspect that an ordering of life that expresses all their own aspirations for happiness may yet fail to win happiness for personalities quite differently constituted. On the other hand, there must come to every thoughtful mind with growing experience a profound appreciation of the preciousness of an existing order. Political change is inevitable, but those nations in which the political instinct has been at work most successfully have always striven to secure for every change the support, in so far as it might be possible, of the sentiments and loyalty that in connection with the previous form of government had helped to bind men together. Such sentiments and loyalty are of slow growth and cannot easily be suddenly called into existence. In proportion as they have their roots deep in the past they are far too valuable to be lost, unless, indeed, one is willing to rely upon force, and take for one's motto: *Oderint dum metuant* (Hate if you will, if only you cower).

We who have faith in the power of education really to educate must believe that Montesquieu was right in saying: " The first motive which ought to impel us to study is the desire to augment the excellence of our nature and to render an intelligent being yet more intelligent." Of the Greeks, whose passionate desire to be intelligent has never been surpassed in the history of the world, M. Maurice Croiset said that they had " judgment in im-

agination, intellect in sentiment, reflection in passion." [20]
To blend these qualities is to achieve a rare balance and
harmony of the intellectual and the emotional mind; but
we must add, if we can, to this accomplishment a sense,
peculiarly realized in the history of Rome, of the limitations which membership in the social organism sets to the
translation into action of that life of the mind. We must
strive particularly, if we are to be true exponents of this
constructive and unifying spirit, to bring into mutual
understanding and coöperation all the human forces that
are now in very contradictory ways trying to make this
world a better place in which to live, contradictory because there is as yet no way known in which minds,
whether young or old, may be at once granted liberty
of thought and refused permission to think incorrectly.
However ardently and persuasively we may present our
own views, we shall probably be at times unable to prevent the adoption of views of which we cannot ourselves
approve. But until we lose faith in the efficacy of intelligence aided by character, if we are open-minded and
willing to learn as well as to teach, if, to cite again the
words of Francis Bacon which I quoted early in this address, we are willing to take from one another " light of
invention and not fire of contradiction, and esteem of the
inquisition of truth as of an enterprise and not as of a
quality or ornament," we may reasonably hope for such
uniformity of opinion and practice as is attainable in a
world in which everyday experience and scientific psychology alike prove to us that all general formulations of
opinion, when they become vital elements in actual living,

---

[20] " L'Hellène a toujours eu de la raison dans l'imagination, de l'esprit dans
le sentiment, de la réflexion dans la passion." — M. Croiset, *Histoire de la littérature grecque* (Paris, Fontemoing & Cie, 1910), I, p. 4.

assume a separate significance due to individual personality and individual experience.

As Tennyson said in the " Morte d'Arthur,"

> The old order changeth, yielding place to new,
> And God fulfills Himself in many ways,
> Lest one good custom should corrupt the world.

VERGIL AND THE IDEALS OF PHI BETA KAPPA[1]

THERE IS in Milton's *Areopagitica* a famous eulogy of the printed word: " A good book is the precious life-blood of a master spirit, embalmed and treasured up on purpose to a life beyond life." To a lover of such books who reflects upon the course of human history and the part played therein by the ideas and attitudes of mind recorded in literature, there must come, I think, even in his most hopeful moods, a certain feeling of sadness. The accumulated treasure of thought and insight is so great; the practical utilization of it for the happy ordering of the life of the world has been relatively so slight. So much of vital import has been discovered only to be forgotten or ignored by succeeding generations. The masterpieces of literature say to us reproachfully: " We have piped unto you and ye have not danced; we have mourned unto you and ye have not lamented." [2] The richness of human experience that has been garnered in prose and poetry seems so clearly to possess the virtue of Ithuriel's spear; if only we were willing to make constant use of it, error and misconception could not possibly continue to impose upon us. Yet the true basis of our civic and international relations still in practice eludes us, and the centuries have produced a mutual understanding that is still, as current events conclusively prove, dangerously incomplete. How often, one asks oneself, must mankind

---

[1] Delivered at Troy, N. Y., before the Upper Hudson Phi Beta Kappa Association, Dec., 1930.
[2] St. Matthew xi. 17; St. Luke vii. 32.

learn at great cost the same lesson? How often in books
that by their imaginative power convince the reason and
win the heart must the true greatness and joy of human
life be shown, before the vision persists and begins to be
realized progressively through organized habit? Have we
perhaps cherished an illusion about the range of the influence exerted by literature in the determination of human
action? Is this influence, after all, chiefly esthetic, and, in
so far as it does affect the thought and action of the world,
is its life transitory? The direct influence of the spoken,
unrecorded word is evidently contemporaneous only; in
the light of actual experience may we still believe with
Milton that a good book has in it the potency of a life beyond life? Martial in one of his epigrams observes that
they do not really write whose books no one reads.[3]
Doubtless there have been mute, inglorious Miltons who
in the daily round of intercourse with their fellows rose to
the height of some great argument and justified the ways
of God to men. But they have left no memorial of themselves, save in the lives, perhaps equally unknown to
fame, that they enlarged and strengthened. Their influence, thus, seems to be narrowly limited and confined to
their own times. Does, then, the Milton whom we rank
among the immortals, the great poet of civil and religious
liberty, really exert today an influence commensurate
with his power to inform? Or is he today a living voice to
the appreciative few, to the rest of the world the shadow
of a great name, praised but not read? If this last be true
of Milton, what shall we say of other great names? What,
in particular, of Vergil?

The world today, a world for the most part impatient
of tradition and of traditional sanctions, acclaims the

[3] iii. 9.

bimillennial anniversary of Vergil's birth. But the question recurs: In so far as he is still read for nonprofessional reasons by mature men and women, is his influence chiefly esthetic or has it power to shape for practical ends the thought, feeling, and action of daily life? Of his consummate artistry there can now be no doubt. The disintegrating criticism of the nineteenth century, a not unnatural result of the application of the historical and comparative method to the study of works of art, has led to a minute reëxamination of Vergil's text, considered both in itself and in its relation to the sources from which the poet drew. The labors of many scholars (among whom may be mentioned *honoris causa* Conington, Nettleship, Sainte-Beuve, Boissier, Sellar, Conway, Heinze, and Rand [4]) have proven the soundness of the earlier and traditional estimate of Vergil's genius, an estimate of which Dante is the most brilliant exponent. As Woodberry, himself one of the most accomplished of literary critics that America has produced, justly said in his exquisite essay on Vergil:

He more than any other poet has been a part of the intellectual life of Europe alike by length of sway and by the multitude of minds he touched in all generations; and among the Latin races he is still the climax of their genius, for charm and dignity, for art and the profound substance of his matter, and for its serious inclusiveness of human life. [5]

Now a susceptibility to the peculiar power of great poetry is perhaps no more communicable than an ear for the subtle harmony of great music; but it would seem to be indisputable that if we have ears to hear, Vergil can give us noble pleasure. Should he, in addition, play such a part

[4] To this list should now (1936) be added Buscaroli and Pease.
[5] George E. Woodberry, "Virgil," in *Great Writers* (The Macmillan Company, 1912), p. 112.

in the intellectual life of today as he has played in the centuries that are gone? Is he able, if we admit him to our hearts, to broaden our horizon, to enlarge and quicken our sympathies with the multifarious and often contradictory phases of human life, to help us to enjoy the companionship of ideas and to prefer the guidance of reason to that of our own personal likes and dislikes? Let us see whether there are elements integrally present in the poet and in his work which will enable us to answer such questions.

Even a pronounced modernist would not be unwilling to admit that two reasons for the study of Latin literature are still valid. In the first place, it expresses the varied interpretation of human life reached by a great nation whose disciplined bravery conquered the known world and whose juristic and administrative genius then slowly worked out the idea of a single imperial nationality for all the diverse peoples of its wide domain. This literature is thus indispensable to the student of the continuity of human institutions. But there is a second reason for its historical importance. Greece, yielding to the sway of Rome, captivated her rude conqueror by the varied beauty of her achievement in art and in letters. The persistent study and assimilation of the technique of these masterpieces developed at Rome during the Republic and the Empire a literature through which for centuries Greek culture was transmitted to the Western world. It may be said of Vergil in all sobriety of phrase that in him more than in any other Latin writer there are incarnated both of these claims of Latin literature upon the thoughtful attention of mankind. On the one hand, he came to be regarded even during his own lifetime as the veritable voice of his people, a voice that expressed with exquisite sensibility and elevation of tone the content of their most inspired moods, their sense in such hours of the loveliness of Italy as Italy is glorified in the *Georgics:* [6]

> Salve, magna parens frugum, Saturnia tellus,
> magna virum;
> Hail, mighty mother of harvests, O land of Saturn,
> Mighty mother of men;

their pride in the nation's past, their hope of a commensurate future, their faith in the mission of Rome as the torchbearer of civilization, as the story of Rome is unfolded in the Fourth *Eclogue* and in the *Aeneid.* Tennyson addresses him as " Roman Virgil." The characterization dates back to the time of Nero, when Petronius Arbiter showed his usual keen literary taste and insight by thus summing up in a single adjective the significance of the poet in his world. On the other hand, no other Latin poet is so widely conversant with Greek authors and makes such constant use of them to achieve his own quite different purposes. For we may note in passing that while not only in form and rhythm, but also in idea, phrase and color, Vergil draws freely upon his models, the spirit and total effect of his work is essentially Roman, not Greek. A minute knowledge of a thousand years of Greek poetry enriched his observation of his own stirring times with an imaginative portrayal of the inner life of man in connection with the problems that eternally imperil human happiness, all described in forms of art by writers who themselves loved and understood the life they pictured. His absorbed studies of these works of the Greek genius greatly quickened in him certain ways of thinking and feeling for which, though typically Greek, he had already,

[6] ii. 173, 174.

I fancy, a natural aptitude. When Socrates says [7] " Let us follow the argument whithersoever it leads," he expresses not merely the spirit of the Platonic philosophy but the deep-seated desire of the Greeks to see things as they really are, no matter what the consequences of the discovery may be. But if, in such a spirit, one endeavors to understand the behavior of human beings, whether as individuals or as members of society, one quickly discovers that the players in life's drama are not personified abstractions. Rarely is the issue clearly joined between acknowledged justice and confessed injustice, as it is, for example, in Bunyan's *Pilgrim's Progress*. Again and again in the pathetic history of human antagonisms both parties to the controversy give ample proof that they sincerely believe their ideas to be true and right both for themselves and for others also. George Eliot says of the parting of Romola and Savonarola, " The two faces were lighted up, each with an opposite emotion, each with an opposite certitude." [8] In such irreconcilable clashes, to agree with both sides is not necessary nor indeed possible; but to understand both sides and to feel the pathos of the fate of the loser is indispensable, unless, indeed, one is prepared, as, alas, thousands of earnest men and women have always been prepared, to stretch life forever upon a Procrustean bed. It is one of the elements of greatness in Vergil that he has so profound a comprehension of the many-sidedness of human life, and that he has so keen a sense of the wretchedness of the loser even when his heart or reason or both are on the side of the winner. Woodberry, indeed, declares that " he was to be the greatest lover in the world of all things beautiful, strong, tender, pitiful, sad and fated."

---

[7] Plato, *Republic* iii. 394 D.   [8] *Romola,* chap. lix.

Let me quote to you in lighter vein an entertaining presentation of a typical clash of interests. The actors, it is true, are animals, but Aesop has made us familiar with the use of such tales to teach a moral lesson. In a book entitled *The Phantom Public,* an attempt to discuss and answer the question " Can the majority rule? " by Dr. Walter Lippmann, an accomplished member of the editorial staff of the *New York World,* I find the following passage: [9]

Darwin's story of the cats and clover (as told by J. Arthur Thomson, *The Outline of Science,* III, 646) may be recommended to anyone who finds it difficult to free his mind of the assumption that his notions of good and bad are universal. The purple clover is cross-fertilized by the bumble bee, and, therefore, the more bumblebees the better next year's crop of clover. But the nests of bumblebees are rifled by field mice which are fond of white grubs. Therefore, the more field mice the fewer bumblebees and the poorer the crop. But in the neighborhood of villages the cats hunt down the field mice. And so the more cats, the fewer mice, the more bumblebees, the better the crop. And the more kindly old ladies there are in the village, the more cats there will be.

If you happen not to be a Hindu or a vegetarian, and are a beef-eating Occidental, you will commend the old ladies who keep the cats who hunt the mice who destroy the bumblebees who make the pasture of clover for the cattle. If you are a cat, you also will be in favor of the old ladies. But if you are a field mouse how different the rights and wrongs of that section of the universe! The old ladies who keep cats will seem about as kindly as witches with pet tigers, and the Old Lady Peril will be debated hysterically by the Field Mouse Security League; for what could a patriotic mouse think of a world in which bumblebees did not exist for the sole purpose of producing white grubs for field mice? There would seem to be no law and order in such a world; and only a highly philosophical mouse would admit with Bergson that, "the idea of disorder objectifies for the convenience of language, the disappointment of a mind that finds before it an order different from what it wants." — (*Creative Evolution,* chap. III). For we recognize as good an order suited to our needs and hopes and habits.

[9] P. 31.

If we return now to Vergil, we note at once that Dido is not philosophical, neither is Turnus. Both are finely drawn characters with hearts set upon the satisfaction of desires that are, in themselves, wholly commendable. In the ruin that comes upon both, the essence of tragedy lies in the fact that their desires are in opposition to a divine purpose in history and that they themselves recognize no other criterion of the rightfulness of action than their own personal likes and dislikes. Both are individualists, though, as is often true of high-minded individuals, each identifies the claims of these likes and dislikes with the demands of a great external cause. Dido, at the opening of the Fourth Book, accepts as valid her sister Anna's plea that it is her duty as Queen to marry this hero Aeneas in order to secure the safety and ultimately the greatness of the new city that she has led her trusting followers into the wilderness to found. Turnus, though, in spite of the warm support of Queen Amata, he has never been formally betrothed to the Princess Lavinia, places himself with impetuous indignation at the head of a coalition of Italian tribes hastily formed to drive out of Italy these alien invaders whose first contact with the people to whom the land belonged resulted in the slaughter that followed upon Ascanius' wounding of Silvia's pet stag, a slaughter which included aged Galaesus, slain as he rushed between the combatants to plead for peace, Galaesus the most righteous of all men in the Ausonian land. Turnus, we may be sure, knows full well that as a lover he far outshines Aeneas in Lavinia's eyes. The union that in the end was consummated was purely dynastic; against this settlement Turnus fought with the fury of a brave and patriotic soul. But, confident as both Dido and Turnus are of the justice of their cause, both in

Vergil's eyes are in the wrong, and must succumb. The atmosphere in which their stories move is that of Greek tragedy. " The plot involves the resistance of individual passion and inclination to the more widely-reaching divine purpose; human passion bent on its own fulfilment in contempt of the gods, and ending, as it can only end, in infatuation and ruin." [10] Now Vergil was profoundly religious. Early in his life he had come, it is true, under the spell of Lucretius. The Sixth *Eclogue* and the Second *Georgic,* not to speak of other evidence, show clearly how intimate must have been his familiarity with Lucretius' great poem. But technical Epicureanism, which denied to the gods all knowledge of human life, was too austere a creed for a nature like Vergil's, innately distrustful of the conclusions of the reason whenever they conflicted with the attachments of the heart, and, as George Eliot said of Daniel Deronda, " loath to part with long-sanctioned forms which for him were quick with memories and sentiments that no arguments could lay dead." [11] Besides, Lucretius was himself religiously minded, so that, as M. Patin has brilliantly shown [12] Lucretius, having by inexorable logic excluded the gods altogether from influence upon human destiny, seems to deify the vital energy of Nature herself in order to satisfy his longing for something divine. Already in the *Georgics,* where the influence of Lucretius is obvious, especially in the sublime passage in which at the close of the Second Book Vergil glorifies the life of the country as contrasted with the life of the town, the poet's thoughts are full of the happy

---

[10] Henry Nettleship, " Suggestions Introductory to a Study of the Aeneid," p. 31. See p. 58 n.

[11] *Daniel Deronda,* chap. xxxii.

[12] " L'Antilucrèce chez Lucrèce," in *Études sur la poésie latine* (Hachette et Cie, 1900), I, 117–37.

round of feasts and thanksgivings to the gods for their protecting care as the seasons in succession bring their appropriate labors and no less appropriate rewards in accordance with a divinely ordered plan. In the *Aeneid* this feeling of the presence and activity of the divine in the forward movement of civilization pervades the entire epic. The poem is in a very real sense a religious poem, as Boissier in his *La Religion romaine* [13] and Nettleship in the essay from which I have already quoted convincingly show. The subject of the *Aeneid* is not merely the centuries of toil and sacrifice through which Rome came to be the mistress of the known world; it is also, and pervasively, the significance of the growth of the Roman Empire as the divinely chosen instrument for the spread among the nations of the earth of the highest civilization that man had achieved. To this far-off event toward which the whole creation then moved, Dido and Turnus place themselves in opposition. In so doing they choose the side that cannot possibly win. But they are personalities of true tragic dignity; they deserve our sympathy, and Vergil intends that they shall receive it. The cases, however, are disparate. Vergil lavishes every resource of his exquisite art upon his portrayal of the pathos of the fate of the Carthaginian queen, and is evidently far more deeply moved by the disastrous result of her opposition to the will of Providence than he is by the tragic end of Turnus, though this is due to a like opposition. In accord with the spirit of Greek tragedy, Vergil draws neither character as flawless. Aristotle regarded the *Oedipus Rex* of Sophocles as the masterpiece of Greek drama; [14] Hegel gave that place to the *Antigone*, [15] but

---

[13] *La Religion romaine*, I, 230–47.
[14] *Poetics*, by implication in many passages.   [15] *Esthetics* iii. 2.

it has been justly said that "Antigone is too austere, too blameless, for the ideal tragic protagonist, who must display some infirmity of purpose, some lapse of piety if he is to arouse the pity and fear of the spectators." [16] If I read the *Aeneid* aright, Vergil marks as the flaw in Dido's otherwise royal character her disregard of the vow to remain faithful to the memory of Sychaeus, a vow solemnly repeated at the beginning of the Fourth Book at the very moment when she feels herself responsive to the new passion, a vow to which later, when her dream of happiness with Aeneas has been shattered, her thoughts sadly recur:

> Non servata fides cineri promissa Sychaeo.
> The faith vowed to the ashes of Sychaeus I have not kept.[17]

She has thus proved false to an obligation which, whatever might be said of its objective validity or invalidity, she herself regarded as binding. With this exception Dido is a magnificent creature, so much so as to suggest that Vergil may almost have fallen in love with his own creation as Pygmalion did with Galatea. Some scholars have thought that the poet had originally in mind Cleopatra and her success in ensnaring Antony. If this was ever true in the first conception of the story, the being whom Vergil's imagination evoked became, as he endeavored to realize her, too fine and noble a character to be used to teach any such lesson. There is not in Dido, I venture to say, a trace of Cleopatra. One utterance alone is sufficient to mark the chasm between the two women:

> Saltem si qua mihi de te suscepta fuisset
> ante fugam suboles, si quis mihi parvulus aula
> luderet Aeneas, qui te tamen ore referret,
> non equidem omnino capta ac deserta viderer.[18]

[16] W. C. Wright, *A Short History of Greek Literature*, p. 223.
[17] iv. 552.   [18] iv. 327–30.

At least, if ere thy flight a child had been born to me by thee, if in
my hall a tiny Aeneas were playing, whose face, in spite of all,
would bring back thine, I should not think myself utterly van-
quished and forlorn.

H. Dessau, in an acute analysis of the available evidence,[19] has made it reasonably certain that the story of
the tragic loves of Dido and Aeneas is original with Vergil himself. In the legendary historical account of Dido
which appears in Justin [20] Aeneas is not mentioned at
all. In that account Iarbas, as in Vergil, is a suitor for
Dido's hand. He threatens that if she refuses him he will
sack her newly founded city and take her by force. Confronted thus by the alternative of either proving false to
her vow of eternal fidelity to her dead husband, or bringing upon her trusting people the horrors of war, she
mounted the funeral pyre and committed suicide. It has
been repeatedly asserted that Naevius introduced the
love story of Aeneas and Dido into his epic on the first
Punic War. But the evidence for this is of the flimsiest
kind, and it is *a priori* incredible that Naevius, writing
his poem before the close of the Hannibalic War, in other
words, before Rome was assured of victory in the war in
which she long stood on the very brink of destruction,
should have imagined that in those years of terror and
hatred he could enhance the appeal of a national epic by
including in it a love story of the Trojan founder of
Rome and the Queen of the city with which Rome was
still locked in deadly combat. Dionysius of Halicarnas-
sus, who was resident in Rome during the years in which
Vergil was engaged upon the *Aeneid,* and for some time
after Vergil's death, published in 7 B.C. his *Antiquitates
Romanae.* In the First Book of this work, he gives from

---

[19] " Vergil und Karthago, Dido und Anna," in *Hermes,* XLIX, 1914, pp.
508–37.   [20] xviii. 7.

the standpoint of an historian an account of the material that is relevant to the wanderings of Aeneas from Troy to the arrival in Italy, an account in which he is again and again in detailed agreement with Vergil. He must have had knowledge of the *Aeneid*, for its fame was already great; yet he says not a word of a landing at Carthage. This silence is comprehensible only on the supposition that he found no hint of Vergil's version in the sources for legend and history which he used and therefore regarded that version as a new bit of fiction. We have, besides, the definite statement of Macrobius [21] that Vergil was the creator of a new and wholly different Dido.

I have dwelt in some detail upon the very great probability, perhaps it is safe to say the substantial certainty, that the encounter of Aeneas and Dido was Vergil's own creation because of its bearing on the long-vexed question of our poet's originality. It is true that his use of material drawn from his predecessors, both Greek and Latin, is obtrusive. While he was still alive, hostile critics were busy with what they bluntly called " Vergil's thieveries." Yet, as a result of his subtle alchemy, the temper and outlook of the *Aeneid* is so Roman, not Greek, that to Vergil's countrymen the hero of the epic seemed to be not Aeneas but the Roman people itself, as is shown in the phrase *Gesta Populi Romani,* currently used to describe it. This difference of personality and spirit between Homer and his alleged imitator has been much elaborated by living Vergilian scholars. Perhaps the most impressive instance may be found in a comparison of the Sixth Book of the *Aeneid* with the Eleventh Book of the *Odyssey,* though one cannot well overlook the difference between the purely human character of the scenes repre-

[21] *Saturnalia* v. 17. 5.

sented on the shield of Achilles and the wholly national character of the scenes represented on the corresponding shield of Aeneas. But if Vergil's portrayal of Dido is really original with himself, he has furnished as striking a proof of creative power as any poet who coveted that reputation could possibly desire.

As I have already said, Dido and Turnus, alike in their opposition to the divine purpose, are yet differently conceived. In Turnus the flaws required by tragedy are numerous. He is violent, arrogant, impatient of divine guidance, ready to break a solemn covenant, absorbed in his own personal ambitions. Yet he is a brave and ardent lover and patriot, and at the close of the single combat in Book XII, Aeneas would have spared his prostrate foe had he not perceived on Turnus' shoulder the belt of youthful Pallas, King Evander's only son, whom Turnus had slain. In the very last line of the whole poem Vergil, who has drawn Turnus throughout as the foil of Aeneas, nevertheless is aware of the tragedy involved in the Rutulian chieftain's untimely death, and thus we have the moving final line:

> Vitaque cum gemitu fugit indignata sub umbras.
> And with a moan life passed indignant to the shades below.

> Our wills are ours, we know not how;
> Our wills are ours, to make them Thine.

Thus wrote Tennyson in the prelude to *In Memoriam*. To the modern world, with its apotheosis of individualism, Aeneas, as Vergil has drawn him, is apt to seem rather a concept than a real human being. Yet he incarnates the virtues upon which, to the poet's mind, depended the realization of the high hopes of the new era. Rome had learned to her cost the meaning of personal

ambition. Vergil held up to his countrymen the contrasted picture of patience, self-control, and obedience to
the divine call. Through such forgetfulness of self, and
through this alone, it had been possible to lay the foundations of the State; through the same high devotion the
commonwealth had grown great. In no other way could
her life be preserved and enriched for the generations to
come.

I know of no finer presentation of Aeneas' character,
as Vergil conceived him, than that of the English historian, J. R. Green, published in 1876 in his *Stray Studies
from England and Italy* under the title: "Aeneas: a
Virgilian Study." Brief as it is (there are only twenty-
three pages) it shows throughout a sympathetic insight
into the poet's intentions and workmanship that would
surely win Vergil's gratitude could he listen to it. But I
cannot forego this opportunity of bringing to your attention the "philosophical Romance," as its author
calls it, that more than any other modern story has
helped me to appreciate in Aeneas, as the growth of his
character is indicated in the poem, the nature and influence of the central motive which in the end enters into
and unifies all the others. If you have read the fascinating romance by J. Henry Shorthouse entitled *John Inglesant,* you will recall that the hero was from early youth
trained with the utmost care to play a particular rôle in
the political and religious life of his times. The scene is
laid in England in the period of the conflict between
Charles I and Parliament, though in the years that followed Cromwell's victory Inglesant lived for the most
part in Italy. He is introduced to the reader as a dreamy,
spiritually minded boy who absorbs Plato and comes to
believe that obedience to the heavenly vision is the very

hallmark of a gentleman. The Papacy was making every effort to win back England, and it was felt to be highly desirable to have the services of men who because of their birth, temperament, and education might be acceptable mediators and be trusted by both parties, and who yet, because they were not extremists, might by the charm of their manner and conversation win support for the party that they represented. Young Inglesant is trained for work of this kind by a Jesuit priest, an accomplished scholar and man of the world, himself an incarnation of the desired type of character. Most of this work was reasonably safe, but the times were critical, especially after the outbreak of the war, and any moment might bring a call to face extreme danger. A single quotation must suffice to suggest to you the kinship of Inglesant and Aeneas. Inglesant is kneeling in the church at Gidding.[22]

He looked up at some noise, and saw, standing in the dark shadow under the west window, the messenger of the Jesuit whom he knew. He got up quietly and went out. From his marriage feast, nay, from the table of the Lord, he would have got up all the same had that summons come to him. His whole life from his boyhood had been so formed upon the idea of some day proving himself worthy of the confidence reposed in him (that perfect unexpressed confidence which won his very nature to a passionate devotion capable of the supreme action, whatever it might be, to which all his training had tended) that to have faltered at any moment would have been more impossible to him than suicide, than any self-contradictory action could have been — as impossible as for a proud man to become suddenly naturally humble, or a merciful man cruel. That there might have been found in the universe a power capable of overmastering this master passion is possible; hitherto, however, it had not been found.

If, with these ideas in mind, we turn to the *Aeneid*, we must note that the character of the hero is, in these re-

22 Chap. xi.

spects, not fully developed at the beginning of the poem. There is a growth due to many formative experiences, the most important being the illumination that comes to him through his visit to the Lower World and what he learns there from his father. Warde Fowler has admirably discussed these changes in Aeneas [23] and there has just appeared a new and even more detailed analysis of these changes by Professor George Howe, of the University of North Carolina.[24] In the last six books, in which the struggle for dominion is waged on the soil of the homeland itself, Aeneas knows no longer what it is to falter. His soul, like Vergil's own, is attuned to vaster harmonies than those of individual happiness. His energies, like Vergil's own, become part of the movement in history that is to produce and maintain a majestic world order of law and peace. The work which he has to do is not of his choosing, and the performance of it brings him slight personal satisfaction. He is usually incarnate loneliness. But he takes refuge in high fortitude and cheers himself with the thought that, as Tennyson says in *Locksley Hall*,

> The individual withers, and the world is more and more.

In view of the announced title of this paper it may seem strange that I have thus far made no reference to Phi Beta Kappa. It is true that no specific mention has been made of our ideals ; nevertheless in a very real sense everything that has been said is relevant to those aspirations of which the key is the outward and visible sign. We stand for character and scholarship, for neither without

[23] W. W. Fowler, *The Religious Experience of the Roman People*, Lecture xviii.

[24] George Howe, " The Development of the Character of Aeneas," in *The Classical Journal*, Dec., 1930.

the other, but for the interplay of both. All the tragedy and all the comedy of human life teach insistently the need of a dispassionate understanding of objective facts, to the end that the conscience may be safely guided. For the pathway of mankind is strewn with cases in which a conscience that would have done credit to an archangel led a human being to acts that ruined the happiness of his fellows, and often of himself as well.[25] On the other hand, knowledge without character suggests a vista of possibilities that brings to mind De Quincey's essay on " Murder as One of the Fine Arts." To be intelligent, then, is an obligation no less binding than to be virtuous, and to be virtuous is an obligation no more binding than to be intelligent. But there are two important differences between the two objectives. The world of conscience can very easily be a small world; the world of knowledge cannot properly be anything but a large world. The world of conscience may very easily be wholly concerned with one's own conception of truth and right; the world of knowledge is necessarily no less concerned with the conceptions of truth and right held by others than with our own personal definition. Vergil's poetry reveals the spaciousness of the world with which his mind was occupied, a world with a rich and thought-provoking past, an epoch-making present, and an illimitable future of hope for the happiness of mankind through the beneficent *pax Romana*. It was the mind of a scholar that thus mused upon the meaning of the pageant of history; it was also a disinterested mind, that exalted Rome not for what she

[25] In *The Phantom Public,* mentioned above, p. 100, Mr. Lippmann, with profound insight, declares (pp. 28 and 29): " It will require more than a good conscience to govern modern society, for conscience is no guide in situations where the essence of the difficulty is to find a guide for the conscience . . . For effective virtue, as Socrates pointed out long ago, is knowledge; and a code of the right and the wrong must wait upon a perception of the true and the false."

had conquered for herself but for what she had already achieved and was still in the future going to achieve in the service of all men, that was naturally inclined to find something of worth on both sides of a question, and was, therefore, distrustful of the rough methods which had hitherto been used to settle questions, that considered with profound sadness the price which had been paid in anguish and death for the progress of civilization, alike by those who won and by those who lost in the clash of opposing ideas. In his scholarship and largeness of vision, in the breadth and intelligence of his sympathy, in his fervent yet hesitant hope of a future era of peace and justice, when Mars shall rage no more and goodwill be omnipresent, Vergil is as fine a representative of the ideals of Phi Beta Kappa as great poetry affords.

May it come to pass that at the arrival of his trimillennial anniversary the world will still acclaim his worth, and that it may assert with pride that since the bimillennial notable progress has been made toward the full realization of his philosophy of life!

HORACE[1]

I

Vixere fortes ante Agamemnona
multi; sed omnes inlacrimabiles
urgentur ignotique longa
nocte, carent quia vate sacro.

THUS DOES HORACE, using in his wonted fashion a specific instance to illustrate a general concept, express the indispensability of a record of human experience and achievement. Long before " the tale of Troy divine " had captivated the ears of the ancient world, other deeds of prowess had been done which failed of their due meed of praise from succeeding generations because they found no chronicler. As the centuries passed, the record of memorable speech and action was notably augmented; but, great as the tradition has now become, it is nevertheless incomplete. If we had the data with which to reconstruct the life histories of these forgotten men, we should find in these additions to the record the same essential tragedy and comedy of human life, the pathos of unmerited defeat, the splendor of heroic accomplishment, the material, in short, of noble literature. The author of *Ecclesiasticus* did well to include in his chapter on the praise of famous men " some who have no memorial, who are become as though they had never been born." Because the requisite data were never recorded, or, if recorded, have perished, they are today " to fortune and to fame unknown."

[1] This paper is a fusion (with some omissions and additions) of two articles, entitled, respectively, " Horatian Criticism of Life " and " Horace," published in the *Columbia University Quarterly* for June, 1917, and for March, 1936.

Nevertheless, the Muses, the daughters of Memory,[2] through whose inspiration worthy records are made of those moments of human excellence which deserve to be held in remembrance, have been gracious to us. From the days of the Cro-Magnons to our own much, it is true, has been lost; but the treasures that have been preserved are such, alike in their variety and in their power to inform and to charm, that we can at will escape from the prison-house of " *was uns alle bändigt, das Gemeine* "[3] and from the limitations of our immediate physical and mental environment into a larger world. The daughters of Memory, the time-binding faculty of man, have created and conserved for us a realm in which " the delight of great books " (as Professor John Erskine has felicitously phrased the title of a fine volume of his essays) makes us independent of time and space. It is fitting, therefore, as the recurrent anniversaries offer occasion, to commemorate the presence on this earth of those men and women of genius who live immortally in that spacious and enchanting realm. And thus our thoughts may now gratefully turn to Horace, who, as he was during his actual life *dulcis amicis,* so is still, after the lapse of two thousand years, the welcome friend and counselor of all who have come to know him through his writings.

II

The celebration of an anniversary, especially of a birthday with which are associated two thousand years of fame, may properly suggest some questions about the

[2] H. J. Rose, *A Handbook of Greek Mythology* (E. P. Dutton & Co., 1929), p. 51. " The next consort [of Zeus] after Demeter was Mnemosyne (Memory) the Titaness. Of her were born the nine Muses . . . This seems to be nothing but allegory; by divine help Memory produces the arts and crafts."
[3] Goethe, *Epilog zu Schillers Glocke.*

nature of Horace's permanent contribution to literature. To what extent is the enjoyment of his verse today chiefly esthetic? To what extent does the outlook on life which he incarnated exercise through this enjoyment a formative influence upon the thought, feeling, and action of those who still read his works?

Our age is impatient of tradition, which it no longer regards as life-sustaining. It is absorbed in the novel sensations of the kaleidoscopic present and in dreams of a still more wonderful future. The past is consigned to historical museums, and, even so, is regarded with curiosity rather than with reverence.

The reading of the great past literature has become a specialty, abandoned with obvious relief by the general reader to the conduct of the selected few. Never probably in the world's annals has nearness in time outweighed such grave defects in the contemporary output, such high superiorities in ancestral merit.[4]

Excessere omnes adytis arisque relictis
di, quibus imperium hoc steterat.[5]

But is it really true that the ancient oracles are no longer responsive to our need? We are profoundly concerned today with the question of the standard of corporate and national ethics. The accomplished editor of the *Hibbert Journal* has recently expressed his conviction that it is a State-nature and not human nature which is responsible for the insanity now raging in Europe. But eighteen centuries ago Tacitus, as Professor Bury [6] has pointed out, " judged actions by the ideals of virtue and nobility, and was not prepared to acknowledge that the standard applied to private conduct may be inapplicable to public

4 O. W. Firkins, " The Cult of the Passing Hour," *Atlantic Monthly*, May, 1914, p. 665.
5 Vergil, *Aeneid* ii. 351, 352.
6 *Ancient Greek Historians*, p. 231.

transactions." And four centuries earlier still, Demosthenes,[7] protesting against a breach of good faith on the part of the commonwealth, had warned the Athenians not to exhibit as a nation conduct which they would shrink from as individuals. Under the guidance of the modern scientific spirit we are learning slowly, very slowly, to distrust the universal validity of our personal beliefs and disbeliefs, however broadly these may be based upon observation and reasoned analysis. The possibilities of our individual brains, however remarkable, are not after all coterminous with the possibilities of the truth. But Aristotle[8] long ago pointed out that " those who would adequately judge the truth must be arbitrators and not litigants," and in these words gave expression not only to his own intellectual temper, but to a characteristic attitude of the best thought of Hellas. Has Horace, who hitherto to each successive age has seemed " to express its own familiar wisdom and experience," now no vital message for our time?

III

I am a believer, then, in the old tradition of the enduring value of that literature, whether of ancient, of medieval, or of modern times, which has been winnowed out by generations of competent critics, and pronounced worthy. This value is not merely nor even chiefly esthetic, but is found in the power of such literature to shape for practical ends the thought and action of daily life. I am old-fashioned enough to accept still De Quincey's famous distinction between the literature of knowledge and the literature of power, and, while regarding both as indis-

---

[7] *In Leptinen* 136.   [8] *De caelo* i. 10.

pensable, to assign the primacy to the latter. Our age, however, prizes most the former, and worships that efficiency which through the wide dispersion and use of this knowledge it believes will be secured as never before in the history of the world. I should be the last to depreciate the inestimable value of modern science. But have we sufficiently considered the obvious fact that the skill into which exact knowledge may be transmuted is simply a means to an end, a tool which is equally at the service of the saint and the sinner, of the altruist and the self-seeker? More than this, through the various forms of organization so characteristic of modern society the power of its possessors is so enormously multiplied that they may with the noblest intentions become a positive menace to civilization as other human beings conceive it. If we could answer Pilate's question and give a definition of truth that would be valid for all men, the case would be different. The increase of knowledge and the intelligent and ever more skillful application of it to the problems of society might then bring us onward in a straight line to a predetermined goal. But we do not know the one best form of organization toward which we should strive. We have no permanently valid thought-model for the realization of which in the conduct of the individual and of the State we may labor. It is in fact increasingly probable, and in the opinion of many already quite certain, that there is no *one* ordering of life that is best for all men.

Consider for a moment a striking example of this question.

Better fifty years of Europe than a cycle of Cathay

said Tennyson, and in so saying expressed a view then and now widely held. But Sir Robert Hart, than whom

no man has ever been more competent to speak, says [9] of
the Chinese:

> They are well-behaved, law-abiding, intelligent, economical, and
> industrious; they can learn anything; they are punctiliously polite,
> they worship talent, and they believe in right so firmly that they
> scorn to think it requires to be supported or enforced by might;
> they delight in literature, and everywhere they have their literary
> clubs and coteries for learning and discussing each other's essays
> and verses; they possess and practise an admirable system of ethics,
> and they are generous, charitable, and fond of good works; they
> never forget a favor, they make rich return for any kindness, and,
> though they know money will buy service, a man must be more
> than wealthy to win public esteem and respect; they are practical,
> teachable, and wonderfully gifted with common-sense; they are
> excellent artisans, reliable workmen, and of a good faith that every-
> one acknowledges and admires in their commercial dealings; in no
> country that is or was, has the commandment " Honor thy father
> and thy mother " been so religiously obeyed, or so fully and without
> exception given effect to, and it is in fact the keynote of their family,
> social, official, and national life, and because it is so " their days are
> long in the land " God hath given them.

Will China really gain more than she will lose by the
introduction of Western ideas and methods? The true
answer to this question, as to a thousand others equally
open and perplexing, is hidden in the future; but the
average forceful mind has already prejudged the decision, and purposes the enforcement of its view. An un-
sympathetic observer might be inclined to impute to such
a mind that supreme egotism which finds in the precise
formulation of its own opinion a necessary kinship with
the final truth. But the judgment would show a lack of
discernment. Rather is it true that the imperious demand
for self-expression insists upon finding a world plastic to
its needs; and the imagination, as yet childlike and
undisciplined, instinctively defines the progress of that

---

[9] " *These from the Land of Sinim,*" *Essays on the Chinese Question* (London,
1901), pp. 141, 142.

world in terms of its own ideals. Perhaps in the end the
life of a nation might be so ordered by the superior wisdom of a governing class that under favorable circumstances the concrete results for happiness might be far
greater than those which could be secured by the experi-
ments of a democracy. If material comfort only were
the end of existence, the loss of individual initiative
might be justified. The modern Esau might actually be
commended for relinquishing his birthright to men con-
fessedly cleverer than he and for eating with humble content the savory pottage which they in their wisdom pro-
vided. If, however, life has a wider significance, one must
feel that it is perilous to resign the essence of its good,

> et propter vitam vivendi perdere causas.[10]

Faust makes with Mephistopheles the compact of every
individual soul with life:

> Werd' ich beruhigt je mich auf ein Faulbett legen,
> So sei es gleich um mich gethan;
> Kannst du mich schmeichelnd je belügen,
> Dass ich mir selbst gefallen mag,
> Kannst du mich mit Genuss betrügen:
> Das sei für mich der letzte Tag!

Ever-growing knowledge and intelligence, ever-widening
horizons, ever-broadening sympathies — these, gained
by a *self-determined* development, are the *verae vivendi
causae*, not the good things of life which today represent
Juvenal's *panem et circenses*. Professor John Dewey has
acutely [11] discussed the difference between two " irrecon-
cilably opposed educational and industrial ideals," between education on the one hand and training on the
other, between " a democratic and a feudal control of
industry." It is true, as he finely says, that

[10] Juvenal viii. 84.
[11] " Learning to Earn," *School and Society,* March 24, 1917.

the curriculum on this narrow trade plan will neglect as useless for
its ends the topics in history and civics which make future workers
aware of their rightful claims as citizens in a democracy, alert to
the fact that the present economic struggle is but the present-day
phase taken by the age-long battle for human liberties. The studies
which fit the individual for the reasonable enjoyment of leisure
time, which develop good taste in reading and appreciation of the
arts, will be passed over as good for those who belong by wealth to
the leisure class, but quite useless in the training of skilled em-
ployees.

The other idea of industrial education aims at preparing every
individual to render service of a useful sort to the community, while
at the same time it equips him to secure by his own initiative whatever place his natural capacities fit him for. It will remember that
the future employee is a consumer as well as a producer, that the
whole tendency of society, so far as it is intelligent and wholesome,
is to an increase of the hours of leisure, and that an education which
does nothing to enable individuals to consume wisely and to utilize
leisure wisely is a fraud on democracy. So far as method is concerned, such a conception of industrial education will prize freedom
more than docility; initiative more than automatic skill; insight
and understanding more than capacity to recite lessons or to exe-
cute tasks under the direction of others.

IV

The chapter that is devoted to Horace in Professor
Mackail's invaluable *Latin Literature* closes with the
following paragraph:

Among the many amazing achievements of the Greek genius in
the field of human thought were a lyrical poetry of unexampled
beauty, a refined critical faculty, and later than the greater thinkers and outside of the strict schools, a temperate philosophy of life
such as we see afterwards in the beautiful personality of Plutarch.
In all these three Horace interpreted Greece to the world, while
adding that peculiarly Roman urbanity — the spirit at once of the
grown man as distinguished from children, of the man of the world,
and of the gentleman — which up till now has been a dominant
ideal over the thought and life of Europe.

In true commemorative mood, we may with propriety
enlarge upon the items thus succinctly stated, and, in

particular, dwell upon certain aspects of Horace's temperate philosophy of life. The content of this philosophy will necessarily in some measure receive our attention, but we shall to a far greater degree be concerned with the attitude of mind out of which it sprang. In justification of this choice, we may quote the words of a living writer, Gilbert K. Chesterton, who in the introduction to the volume of essays entitled *Heretics* declares:

There are some people, nevertheless — and I am one of them — who think that the most practical and important thing about a man is still his view of the universe. We think that for a landlady considering a lodger, it is important to know his income, but still more important to know his philosophy. We think that for a general about to fight an enemy, it is important to know the enemy's numbers, but still more important to know the enemy's philosophy. We think the question is not whether the theory of the cosmos affects matters, but whether, in the long run, anything else affects them.

Certainly in Horace " the years that bring the philosophic mind " fostered generously those habits of thinking and feeling in which is implicit the secret of his permanent appeal, " perpetually imitated and perpetually inimitable." [12] Because of this characteristic vein of mingled reflection and sentiment he is a definite personality, and " to each successive age or century he has seemed to express its own familiar wisdom and experience. To Montaigne, Addison and Johnson, as to our own times, he speaks with the voice of a familiar friend." [13] He is thus, in a sense, timeless, at once ancient and modern, in spite of the fact that historically he was the product of a specific civilization in a specific period of history.

The world into which Horace was born, December 8, 65 B.C., two thousand years ago, was already old, already rich in experience of organized forms of human society

12 J. W. Mackail, *Classical Studies*, p. 87.
13 W. Y. Sellar, *Horace and the Elegiac Poets*, p. 4.

and of the fine arts of civilization. We can today trace its
antecedents, far more reliably than was possible for Horace himself, through the great centers of culture: Mem-
phis and Thebes in Egypt; Babylon, Nineveh, and Per-
sepolis in the Orient; Cnossus in the Aegean — until
Athens incarnates Hellenic ideas and their realization,
and Alexandria becomes the center of Hellenistic life and
thought. Finally, Rome, " the heir of all the ages, in the
foremost files of time," spread, through her far-flung dominion over the whole Mediterranean area, her ideals of
law and peace, and became the transmitter of Greek
achievement to future generations because, as Horace
says, Latium fell completely under the spell of Greek
thought and imagination.[14] Through Horace's native en-
dowment and natural bent, through his education at
Rome and later at Athens, then already, in a sense, a
university town, he made at home in his receptive, capacious and many-sided mind the artistic forms and content of centuries of Greek poetry and prose, from Homer
onwards. Like all educated Romans he was bilingual,
and, to a far greater extent than most of his countrymen,
cosmopolitan. Nevertheless, wide as are his sympathies
with all noble human life as such — in the penultimate
Ode of Book I he cannot refrain from enthusiastic praise
of Cleopatra's heroic death — he is at heart a genuine
Roman, albeit of a Hellenized type, he is, in fact, quite
definitely a product of his heredity and his time, the clos-
ing years of the great Republic and the formative period
of the new Empire under the competent leadership of
Augustus and Maecenas. A distinguished French critic,
M. Alexis Pierron, declares that Vergil, had he been born

---

[14] *Graecia capta ferum victorem cepit et artes
intulit agresti Latio. — Epp.* ii. 1. 155, 156.

fifty years earlier and so a contemporary of Lucilius, or fifty years later and so a contemporary of Seneca, would still have been Vergil, though not, it is true "*le grand Virgile*." But of Horace this cannot be said. "*Aucun caprice de l'imagination ne saurait le transporter hors de son siècle . . . Horace est, si je l'ose ainsi dire, le siècle d'Auguste en personne. Il en est du moins l'image fidèle et ses écrits en sont le complet miroir.*" [15] If, however, one considers attentively Horace's traits of character, especially that independence of thought, feeling, speech, and action which is revealed in all his work, one may make upon this claim of M. Pierron the comment, that fortunately all of Horace's early manhood belongs to the period when the Republican freedom of speech and action was still everywhere active. In so far as he incarnates and expresses the Augustan Age, he is a friend and champion whose opposition and lingering doubts have been overcome by a slowly maturing conviction that the new régime is not only tolerable but really admirable. In the formation of this conviction he must have been greatly helped by his close intimacy with Maecenas, the able prime minister to whose sagacity and moderation Augustus owed so much. Although Horace takes pains to disclaim any participation in, or even any knowledge of, the discussion and formulation of governmental policies (he insists that his relations with Maecenas are wholly personal and literary, and in no way political), he could not but gain from this close friendship a most favorable impression of the trained judgment, the foresight, and the devotion to the public welfare which were characteristics of Maecenas' personality. In attempting to understand the connection between Horace and his environ-

[15] A. Pierron, *La Littérature romaine,* pp. 404, 405.

ment we may, in fact, go farther. The *Odes,* no less than the *Satires* and *Epistles,* afford ample evidence that he numbered among his friends many men of distinction who, when the battle of Actium finally brought to an end the long-protracted and ruinous civil strife, coöperated with the administration in those various phases of reconstructive work which today we might group under the heading NRA and numerous related alphabetical combinations. Intimacy with such men must have aided in strengthening the confidence that gradually (he was no turncoat, no Vicar of Bray) he came to feel in the changed form of government against which, in the heyday of youth, he had fought at Philippi.

To the *Odes,* certainly, rather than to the *Satires* or the *Epistles* Horace owes his immortality. It is true that in the *Satires* he displays engagingly his powers as a disinterested observer and critic of life, acute, entertaining, and with the passing of the years more and more urbane. He tells us that he owed to his father (to whom, indeed, albeit his father was a mere freedman, he affectionately attributes all that is good in his own character) the formation of a definite habit of noting reflectively the behavior of his fellow-beings. But his father simply fostered the development of a tendency which was congenital. He had a remarkably acute and observant mind. His natural quarry was human nature, in the study of which, his own included, he displayed throughout his life a keen and unfailing interest. His earliest efforts in the field of satire betray, as one might expect, the resentment against society felt by a hot-tempered young enthusiast whose cherished dreams of a bright future had vanished in the crushing defeat of his party at Philippi. He was for a while a kind of Ishmaelite. But acquaintance with Vergil and Varius (acquaintance which soon deepened into friendship) and the resultant admission to companionship and presently close intimacy with Maecenas brought a sunshine into his life that is reflected in a change of tone in his verse. The true Horace reappears, and Maecenas' gift of the Sabine Farm completed the cure. Two of the *Satires* have always been special favorites, the ninth of Book I, in which he tells us how with ironic but punctilious courtesy he tried to defend himself against the unscrupulous importunity of the nameless social climber whom he encountered on the Sacred Way, and the sixth of Book II, in which he sings the praises of the simple life at the Sabine Farm in contrast with the busy but unsatisfying activities of the city, and points his moral by the delightful tale of the Town and the Country Mouse. The *Epistles,* written later and after the *Odes,* show in the author's consummate mastery of style, phrase and metrical smoothness the results of the seven years spent in the meticulous endeavor to achieve perfection of form, diction, and imaginative thought under the strictly defined and inexorable limitations fixed by the laws of the Greek lyric meters which he was ambitious to be the first to use successfully in Latin poetry. The two long letters of Book II represent perhaps the nearest approach to absolute perfection that the Latin language is capable of in this literary *genre.* In the *Epistles,* some apparently genuine missives, others evidently philosophical or literary essays cast in the epistolary form, there is revealed the quintessential Horace, observant, intelligent, sympathetic, humorous, ironic, urbane, unassuming, philosophic. The total charm is so great that some admirers of our poet have been more captivated by it than by the artistry and reflective vein of the *Odes.*

Nevertheless, Horace's own confident prediction of his immortality (*Non omnis moriar*) is made in the poem which forms the *Envoi* to the little volume of 88 lyrics published by him in 23 B.C. and the subsequent centuries have justified his own appraisal of his special merit. If one reads these stanzas in almost any one of the numerous and constantly multiplying translations (for to essay a translation is an almost irresistible temptation) one may find it somewhat difficult to understand why the *Odes* became and have remained so famous. Shelley says of the skylark:

> Like a poet hidden
>   In the light of thought,
> Singing hymns unbidden,
>   Till the world is wrought
> To sympathy with hopes and fears it heeded not.

Horace, on the contrary, selects for his themes aspects of life that, in so far as they are not distinctively Roman and national (there is an impressive number of national Odes), are so familiar as to seem obvious and almost trite. Listen to a list of the non-national themes as you will find it printed in the Introduction to the late Professor Paul Shorey's remarkable edition of the *Odes* and *Epodes:*

That life is short, that the bloom of the rose is brief, that the bird of time is on the wing, that death comes to pauper and prince alike, that it is pleasant to be young and in love, but that you "know the worth of a lass once you have come to forty year," that good wine promotes good fellowship but must be used in moderation, that the bow always bent makes Apollo a dull god, that we cannot escape ourselves, that black care sits behind the horseman, that the golden mean is best, that contentment passes wealth, that he who ruleth his spirit is greater than he who sits on the throne of Cyrus, that patience makes easy what we cannot alter, that brave men lived before Agamemnon, that 'tis sweet and seemly to die for the fatherland — such are the eternal commonplaces that Horace is ever murmuring in our ears.

If the *motiven* on which Horace thus plays variations are so completely the stuff of which normal life is woven, why is their charm so potent and unfailing? Chiefly, as has been pointed out again and again, because of his incomparable artistry in the choice of diction and cadence. He is one of the greatest of phrase-makers. If you have read the late Mrs. Anne C. E. Allinson's delightful little volume of Roman stories entitled *Roads from Rome,* you will recall that her treatment of Horace has the caption " The Phrase-Maker."

It is the possession of this power to choose unerringly the right word and phrase that enabled Horace to write in the *Odes* genuine poetry. Let me quote an apposite passage from one of the latest attempts to define poetry. In May, 1933, Professor A. E. Housman of the University of Cambridge, one of the most brilliant classical scholars that England has produced, and certainly a true poet if there ever was one, delivered at Cambridge the annual Leslie Stephen Lecture, on *The Name and Nature of Poetry.* In the development of his subject he spoke, at one point, as follows:

When I examine my mind and try to discern clearly in the matter, I cannot satisfy myself that there are any such things as poetical ideas. No truth, it seems to me, is too precious, no observation too profound, and no sentiment too exalted to be expressed in prose. The utmost that I could admit is that some ideas do, while others do not, lend themselves kindly to poetical expression; and that these receive from poetry an enhancement which glorifies and almost transfigures them, and which is not perceived to be a separate thing except by analysis.

" Whosoever will save his life shall lose it, and whosoever will lose his life shall find it." That is the most important truth which has ever been uttered, and the greatest discovery ever made in the moral world; but I do not find in it anything which I should call poetical. On the other hand, when Wisdom says in the Proverbs "He that sinneth against me wrongeth his own soul; all they that hate me, love death," that is to me poetry, because of the words in which the idea is clothed; and as for the seventh verse of the forty-ninth Psalm in the Book of Common Prayer, "But no man may deliver his brother, nor make agreement unto God for him," that is to me poetry so moving that I can hardly keep my voice steady in reading it. And that this is the effect of language I can ascertain by experiment: the same thought in the Bible version, "None of them can by any means redeem his brother, nor give to God a ransom for him," I can read without emotion. Poetry is not the thing said but a way of saying it.[16]

It is for this reason that the *Odes* almost defy adequate translation. The statement of the essential theme can, of course, be transferred to another language, but the magical emotional power of the original phrase in its musical metrical setting is too elusive to be precisely reproduced in a different linguistic medium and a different meter. A translation of an Ode may be a fine English poem, but, from the point of view mentioned by Mr. Housman, it will usually differ from Horace in a subtle but very genuine way in its power to stir feeling. Certain it is that, while translations of the *Odes* are very numerous, the consensus of expert opinion is that success on any large scale is still to be achieved. In fact, even in Latin itself, no other Roman poet ever wrote Sapphics or Alcaics (Horace's two favorite measures) that could in artistic excellence compare with his.

If now we turn from the details of Horace's achievement, and endeavor to define and appraise the significance of his personality, considered as a whole, certain things, I think, may be said with great propriety.

Horace is, in the first place, a fine representative of one

[16] *The Name and Nature of Poetry* (The Macmillan Company, 1933), pp. 34, 35.

of the permanently possible attitudes of the human mind
toward its environment. It may seem hazardous to
predicate permanence of any trait of human nature
at a time when it is so vigorously urged on scientific
grounds [17] that " a great part of what has been mistaken
for *nature* is really *nurture,* direct and indirect, conscious, or more commonly, wholly unconscious," and
that " those things therefore that the radical would alter
and the conservative defend are not traits of human nature, but artificial achievements of human nurture." But
there are some fundamental differences between human
beings that I venture to think no changes brought about
by nurture will eliminate from the world. Vergil, for example, was for a time under the spell of Lucretius. But
the two natures were essentially diverse; the one passionately convinced of the supreme efficacy of rigorous thinking, the other innately distrustful of the conclusions of
the reason whenever they conflicted with the attachments
of the heart, and, as George Eliot says of Daniel Deronda, " loath to part with long-sanctioned forms which
for him were quick with memories and sentiments that
no argument could lay dead." [18] Protestantism and
Catholicism are not merely two different forms of worship; they are the outcome of two ultimately different
attitudes of the aspiring soul. There is as yet no warrant
for believing that the subtle essence which we call personality will ever become standardized in the race as a whole.
However completely the facts of nature, in all the possible senses of that highly ambiguous word, shall become
scientifically known, different personalities will attach to

[17] J. H. Robinson, " The Spirit of Conservatism in the Light of History," in
The New History (The Macmillan Company, 1912), pp. 253, 254.
[18] Chap. xxxii.

these facts in any given equation a varying spiritual significance, and thus obtain different answers to the same
problem. Consider, for example, the extraordinary diversity of the results of reverent investigation which Professor McGiffert some years ago set forth in his notable
volume, *The Rise of Modern Religious Ideas*. The study
of the history of philosophy suggests with increasing
force that the great value of philosophical inquiry is to be
found, not in the growing light thrown upon a far distant,
but surely emerging definite goal, but rather in the working out in rational and coherent form of a great variety of
interpretations of life's mystery whereby fundamentally
different souls can live. Such systems, once developed,
would be in their essential elements forever after available for those minds whose spiritual needs they satisfy.

In the second place, the general attitude of mind which
Horace represents is congenial to the ideal spirit of democracy, and the particular form that he himself gives
to it most pertinent to the need of our own age. He is essentially an independent thinker, not only by nature incapable of accepting views upon the authority of others,
but possessed of a mind so open to new ideas and interpretations of life that even his own authority gave him
only provisional warrant for belief. In the first letter of
the first Book of *Epistles*, written when he was over forty
years old, he gives very clear expression to this suspen-
sion of final judgment:

Nunc itaque et versus et cetera ludicra pono;
quid verum atque decens curo et rogo, et omnis in hoc sum;
condo et compono quae mox depromere possim.
Ac ne forte roges quo me duce, quo Lare tuter,
nullius adductus iurare in verba magistri,
quo me cumque rapit tempestas, deferor hospes.
Nunc agilis fio et mersor civilibus undis,

virtutis verae custos rigidusque satelles;
nunc in Aristippi furtim praecepta relabor,
et mihi res, non me rebus, subiungere conor.[19]

He seems, indeed, to have been especially drawn to Aristippus by the latter's flexibility and sunny cheerfulness in the face of untoward circumstances, his ability to be master of things, not mastered by them. In another letter we find the remark:

Omnis Aristippum decuit color et status et res,
temptantem maiora fere, praesentibus aequum.[20]

Much later, in the eighteenth century, Montesquieu speaks of himself in terms that might well be used of this trait in Aristippus: *Ma machine est si heureusement construite, que je suis frappé par tous les objets assez vivement pour qu'ils puissent me donner du plaisir, pas assez pour qu'ils puissent me causer de la peine.*[21]

But neither Cyrenaicism nor any other of the recognized schools could hold Horace permanently. Every school of philosophy tends to present a closed system, which it builds upon a number of axiomatic assumptions through a series of propositions and their corollaries, logically derived from these assumptions. Horace had a mind too interrogative and too distrustful to remain contentedly within any closed system. As he grew older he kept his receptiveness unimpaired. He could say, with Solon,

γηράσκω δ'αἰεὶ πολλὰ διδασκόμενος.
I grow old, always learning many things.

The feeling for proportion, which in the plastic arts is fundamental, he carried over into his studies of the fine art of living. His *aurea mediocritas*, though he was aware he owed it to the Greeks, was nevertheless nothing exter-

---

[19] *Epp.* i. 1. 10–19.
[20] *Ibid.*, i. 17. 23, 24.   [21] *Pensées diverses. Portrait de Montesquieu.*

nal, but rather an engrafted second nature, if not indeed
the natural flowering under proper educational cultivation of his first. Once while staying at Praeneste he re-
read Homer and found him to be a clearer and better
teacher of morals than the professors of Stoicism and the
New Academy. And on another occasion he turns to the
homespun wisdom of Ofellus, once the owner of the farm
on which, after misfortune came, he worked with coura-
geous serenity for another. Horace is essentially an experimental philosopher observing and analyzing the actions of men and their results in society with a view to the
discovery of something better. In this attempt he is confronted by the difficulty that the motives which lie back
of the acts of others are not easy to discover or to evalu-
ate. He considers, therefore, the one person whose motives lie, as it were, as an open book before him, viz., himself; but he does this in the full conviction that he is a
typical human being, one of the many, a curious and
interesting combination of excellences and defects, of
strength and weakness, of reason and unreason. One may
use of him the words which Sidney Colvin uses of Robert
Louis Stevenson in his introduction to the latter's *Vailima Letters:*

> Stevenson belonged to the race of Montaigne and the literary
> egotists. The word seems out of place, since of egotism in the sense
> of vanity or selfishness he was of all men the most devoid; but he
> was nevertheless a watchful and ever interested observer of the
> motions of his own mind. He saw himself, as he saw everything (to
> borrow the words of Mr. Andrew Lang), with the lucidity of
> genius, and loved to put himself on terms of confidence with his
> readers.

This interest in the ordering of life as a fine art is unceasing, and the method is always that of the observer
who studies the past and the present with reference not

to the establishment of a consistent and interrelated theory or system of philosophy to which one may conform
one's daily life, but rather with a view to guidance in trying out new policies which in turn will, he knows, raise
new problems of detail. It does not appear that he ever
even looked forward to the time when he should have
worked out a consistent system of thought. It is true that
he praises consistency and expresses a desire to become
consistent. But life, to whose teaching he was swiftly responsive, was continuously revealing to him the futility
of attempting to imprison the essence and potential development of life in a set of definitive formulas. The very
manner in which he presents his thoughts to his reader is
in harmony with this temperamental attitude. It has frequently been pointed out that he is not a systematic
thinker; and, inasmuch as the majority of mankind desire an orderly sequence and cogent demonstration of the
soundness of a given point of view, Horace has by many
been criticized for lack of coherence or accused of intellectual laziness because he did not think out to their
natural conclusions the implications of his argument. I
venture to think, however, that it is not quite fair to expect from a man who has reached no conclusion a lucid
exposition of the thing that for him does not yet exist.

But the true reason is probably to be found in another
circumstance. Horace's own name for his *Satires* was
Sermones, and while the *Epistles* are letters in form, they
are really a second series of *Sermones.* Both, then, are
talks, not debates. He is working out a philosophy; he
therefore discusses rather than argues. One feels the atmosphere of the give and take of real conversation, the
presence of open-mindedness, the absence of dogmatism.
Doubtless in a perfect world in which the thought and

action of human beings were controlled by high intelligence, *a priori* reasoning might be sound. One might then apply general principles to the daily life of a community without fear of disastrous consequences. But in reality the world is not thus perfect, nor is the widespread exercise of intelligence its characteristic. We do not live in that " dry light " of which Heraclitus spoke, but in a haze, sometimes roseate but more frequently grey, of personal prejudices and predilections. Is it reasonable, Horace would say to us, that in such a world an individual thinker, product as he is of his environment and therefore limited by it, should feel absolutely sure that he, beyond other men, has found the one true way for all? Does a man normally reach and hold conclusions that arise, not from his own capacity to observe and understand, but from the capacity of others with whom he sympathizes, if at all, very imperfectly? But if his thought thus necessarily bears the distinctive impress of his own personality and not that of another — for he cannot escape himself — is it consistent with his dignity as a rational being to assume in advance of experiment that his particular answer to a disputed question is the best for all men? If one man may assert this, why not another? In the conflict of authority, what should decide? General principles, logically applied? Horace's answer is: Life; " by their fruits ye shall know them." You recall the close of the story of Philippus and Mena:

> Qui semel aspexit quantum dimissa petitis
> praestent, mature redeat repetatque relicta.
> Metiri se quemque suo modulo ac pede verum est.[22]

Horace, therefore, as I have said, discusses rather than argues with his reader. One gets everywhere in these

[22] *Epp.* i. 7. 96–98.

" talks " the impression of a free play of ideas. The issue
is not forced, for Horace himself holds the views that he
is presenting subject to such changes as further experience and reflection may bring. His tone and at times his
words suggest a readiness to consider such changes at
once. The letter to Numicius, for example, closes with the
words:

> Vive, vale. Si quid novisti rectius istis,
> candidus imperti; si nil, his utere mecum.[23]

But Horace does not only cherish his own independence; he is scrupulously careful to accord the same privilege to others. He is continuously making available for
others the results of his own self-examination and commending these results to them as worthy of their attention as disinterested studies of the nature of a typical
human being. But the implication of his manner is always such as to leave the acceptance or rejection of the
suggestions offered to the good pleasure of the person
with whom he is talking. It is not merely a question of
good taste and urbanity; it is rather also a question of
fair play. He will not invade another's territory. Always
himself seeking to understand that ever-changing life
which defies any final expression, he finds it impossible to
exert pressure upon others in favor of views which may
after all turn out to be somewhat inadequate. If his ideas
are to be adopted by others, it must be because others as
well as he find those ideas inherently reasonable.

In the maintenance of both the positions which I have
described, his own independence and his unwillingness
to impair in others a like independence, he was power-
fully aided by an element in his nature which is so pervasive as to affect almost everything that he did. That sense

[23] *Ibid.*, i. 6. 67, 68.

of humor, which in its value for the sane ordering of life
may certainly be regarded as second only to a sense of
morality, never deserts him. Yet he is by no means lacking in seriousness. In the early part of his life he was even
enthusiastic, as may be seen from the ardor with which
he embraced the cause of Brutus at Athens and from that
Epode in which he pictures a continuing life of the lost
cause of the Republic in the Islands of the Blest. But
the ardent dreams of that youthful period faded presently " into the light of common day "; and, when later
in middle life and in full harmony with the state policies
of the leader against whom he had fought at Philippi he
wrote the great series of national Odes that open the Third
Book, the feeling, while still strong, is disciplined by that
abiding distrust of excessive hope or emotional idealiza-
tion which came to him from the unceasing endeavor to
see the facts of life as they really are, however little they
may be what one would like to have them. The play of
humor is so constant as to constitute one of the special
charms of his writing, as it must have constituted one of
the special charms of his living personality. He shifts
from jest to earnest and from earnest to jest so swiftly
and so subtly that it is often very difficult to discern
whether he is serious or humorous in what he says. He
has thus the unfailing attraction of a problem that is
never solved, of a secret that is never quite discovered. As
I have said, the amusement with which he views the
course of events is perfectly compatible with an underly-
ing seriousness. He is by no means a Laodicean, but he
gradually became quite sure that from a purely practical
point of view the realization of life's possibilities would
be surer and more complete if one did not prize them too
highly nor stake all one's peace of mind upon their at-

tainment in specific ways at specific times or in specific
forms. The disparity between the intensity of human unhappiness and the often slight, ephemeral, and sometimes wholly imaginary causes of that unhappiness will
dispose one to smile or to grieve as one may be cast in the
mold of a Democritus or of a Heraclitus. Horace, whose
philosophy was always as practical as the early teaching
of his practical father, saw a greater constructive force in
smiles than in tears. And so when he smiles, he does
not look down upon the situation which has caused his
amusement, but rather sympathizes with it. His sense of
humor, operating as it does to save him from over-esti-
mating the value of his own theories, becomes a positive
element in enabling him to present those theories persuasively.

His admirer Persius later epitomized in two verses his
peculiar power:

> Omne vafer vitium ridenti Flaccus amico
> tangit et admissus circum praecordia ludit.[24]

His is the true genius of the comic, " the genius of
thoughtful laughter," [25] the laughter that understands,
that is not unaware of the pathetic side. " Genuine humor
and true wit," says Landor in one of his *Imaginary Conversations,* " require a sound and capacious mind, which
is always a grave one." [26] Horace is profoundly interested
in the fruitful application of ideas to everyday life; he is
profoundly convinced of the value of constructive ideas
and ideals. He laughs or smiles not at these, but at childish misconceptions of them and at the resultant futility
of human effort. To observe this spectacle in a mood

---

[24] i. 116, 117.
[25] George Meredith, *An Essay on Comedy and the Uses of the Comic Spirit*
(Charles Scribner's Sons, 1911), p. 82.
[26] " Alfieri and the Jew Salomon."

wholly serious, to try to change it for the better without
the help of " that modulating and restraining balance-
wheel which we call a sense of humor," is to incur, he
thinks, a grave risk of doing more harm than good. For
seriousness not tempered by humor is prone to over-esti-
mate the efficacy of particular general ideas at particular
junctures. Is thoroughness always commendable? That
depends upon time and place and persons. The decision
must be made not in an ideal world, but for human beings that are as yet in myriad diverse ways imperfect;
and therefore the prudent sociologist, like the prudent
physician, must suit the strength of his healing remedy to
the particular person or group under the particular conditions that obtain. One thing, and one thing only, is
normally certain, that any principle whatever may work
disaster, if it be carried to its logical conclusion and applied because it is theoretically sound.

> Insani sapiens nomen ferat, aequus iniqui,
> ultra quam satis est virtutem si petat ipsam.[27]

That a man devoid of a sense of humor is apt to over-esti-
mate his own importance in the general scheme of things
has been generally admitted; it has not been so generally
perceived that this sense is indispensable to success in
social therapeutics. John Galsworthy has shown us in his
fine novel *The Freelands* how difficult it is to bring ideas
to bear effectively upon a complicated social problem,
and how in the passionate endeavor to secure justice for
one's fellow-beings one may actually do them great in-
jury. If one then admits the propriety of the plea, " I must
be cruel, only to be kind," there is practically no bar-
barity, as current events still prove, that one may not

---

[27] *Epp.* i. 6. 15, 16.

commit with a good conscience. Conservative and radical alike may justly be charged with this narrow-mindedness and its resultant cost to human happiness.

Humanity has made a certain advance in civilization; it hopes to make in the future a still greater advance. It has paid for its present achievement a sum total of human suffering that is beyond computation; must the same terrible price be paid for the achievement that is to come? I fear that the answer will be in the affirmative *unless* education and reflection shall very greatly increase the number of those who cheerfully concede to their fellows the right to be different from themselves without loss of esteem. But this will be quite possible if men will cease to identify naïvely their own personal beliefs with necessary truth, because they have come to understand that in actual life all definitions of " good " are experimental only. The one thing, in fact, that must be jealously safeguarded is liberty to frame and test in practice such experimental definitions.

> Nil admirari prope res est una, Numici,
> solaque quae possit facere et servare beatum.[28]

A Horace, whether of the first century B.C. or of the twentieth century A.D., who thus speaks, will not think himself and his personal ideas quite indispensable to the governing of his world. He will contemplate *leni risu* even his own earnestness in urging others to consider those ideas. And both for himself and for others he will prize so highly the right of individual decision, that he can say in all courtesy to such a listener:

> Quodsi cessas aut strenuus anteis,
> nec tardum opperior nec praecedentibus insto.[29]

[28] *Ibid.*, i. 6. 1, 2.   [29] *Ibid.*, i. 2. 70, 71.

As, from the depths of our grateful hearts, we wish our poet a third millennium of happiness among that

> choir invisible
> Of those immortal dead who live again
> In minds made better by their presence,

we may ask Andrew Lang to be our spokesman in our parting salutation:

Farewell, dear Horace; farewell, thou wise and kindly heathen; of mortals the most human, the friend of my friends and of so many generations of men.[30]

[30] A. Lang, *Letters to Dead Authors,* p. 34.

LATIN EXAMINATIONS AS TESTS
OF INTELLIGENCE[1]

AMONG THE ROMANCES of my early reading that linger pleasantly in my memory is Mrs. Harriet Beecher
Stowe's *Oldtown Folks*. It is a simple yet vivacious description of life in New England as the eighteenth century gave place to the nineteenth, and it appealed to
my imagination then, as in certain moods it does still,
through its pictures of the part that religion, or rather,
perhaps, theology, played in the daily life and thought of
those times. One of the most engaging figures is a certain
Jonathan Rossiter, the head of an academy at which the
four young people of the story are educated. Nearly one
hundred pages are devoted to the experiences of the years
that they spend under his instruction, but a single quotation may serve to suggest the intellectual atmosphere of
their school world.

He scorned all conventional rules in teaching, and he would not
tolerate a mechanical lesson, and took delight in puzzling his pupils
and breaking up all routine business by startling and unexpected
questions and assertions. He compelled everyone to think, and to
think for himself. "Your heads may not be the best in the world,"
was one of his sharp off-hand sayings, "but they are the best God
has given you and you must use them for yourselves."

To tell the truth, he used his teaching somewhat as a mental
gratification for himself. If there was a subject he wanted to investi-
gate, or an old Greek or Latin author that he wanted to dig out, he
would put a class on it, without the least regard to whether it was
in the course of college preparation or not, and if a word was said

[1] A paper read at the fourteenth annual meeting of the Classical Association
of New England, at Wheaton College, Norton, Mass., March 29, 1919. Reprinted
from *The Classical Journal*, May, 1919.

by any poor mechanical body, he would blast out upon him with a sort of despotic scorn. " Learn to read Greek perfectly," he said, " and it's no matter what you read "; or, " learn to use your own heads, and you can learn anything." [2]

We read presently that it was a matter of pride with Mr. Rossiter that his boys should go to Cambridge more than ready, and we are not surprised. His whole training aimed at the development of alert intelligence and individual initiative in the use of it.

However modest we may be, the present war has given us just ground for pride in the intelligence of the American soldier. His resourcefulness has been much in evidence. And certainly never before has the science of psychology been so utilized to ascertain the fact and the degree of the presence of intelligence with a view to securing by proper assignment to duty the greatest military efficiency. The tests [3] used in the army were prepared by a committee of the American Psychological Association and of the National Research Council, and up to November 1, 1918, approximately 1,500,000 men had been tested. Professor E. L. Thorndike has given us recently [4] a very interesting account of some of the results of these tests. He raises the question: " If for the sake of war we can measure roughly the intelligence of a third of a million soldiers a month, and find it profitable to do so, can we not each year measure the intelligence of every child coming ten years of age and will not that be still more profitable? "

It is important to note at this point that the tests used

2 Chap. xxxiii.

3 *Army Mental Tests* (Nov. 22, 1918). Office of the Surgeon General, Washington, D. C.

4 " Scientific Personnel Work in the Army," *Science*, XLIX (Jan. 17, 1919), pp. 53–61.

in the army were intended to measure one thing only, namely, intelligence.

The rating a man earns furnishes a fairly reliable index of his ability to learn, to think quickly and accurately, to analyze a situation, to maintain a state of mental alertness, and to comprehend and follow instructions. The score is little influenced by schooling. Some of the highest records have been made by men who had not completed the eighth grade.[5]

"The score," it is officially claimed, "is little influenced by schooling." It would, however, I should think, be discouraging to feel that study in school or in college dulled the edge of this native intelligence. It would, in fact, seem to be quite unfortunate if any subject in the curriculum should be so taught as not to call into play for the quicker mastery of its problems this general responsiveness to the facts of life. We Latinists certainly must hold with Matthew Arnold [6] that Montesquieu was right in saying that " the first motive which ought to impel us to study is the desire to augment the excellence of our nature and to render an intelligent being yet more intelligent." We must agree with Professor Barrett Wendell when, in an article [7] justifying by purely practical considerations the old system of classics and mathematics in comparison with anything newer, he says:

Education is a matter partly of information and partly of training. The latter phase of it seems to me the more important. A satisfactorily educated man distinguishes himself from an uneducated one chiefly because for general purposes his faculties are better under his control. An educated man, in short, when confronted with new or unexpected problems, can generally use his wits better than an uneducated one. Here we are on purely practical ground.

[5] *Army Mental Tests*, p. 5.

[6] *Culture and Anarchy*, chap. i.

[7] " Our National Superstition," *North American Review*, CLXXIX (1904), pp. 388–401.

If, then, the study of Latin actually furthers the use of one's wits, actually renders a pupil more resourceful when confronted by a problem within the general range of his physical and mental experience, one may reasonably expect to find satisfactory evidence of this throughout the years of the Latin course, and in particular in the examinations in which he has opportunity to use alike his information and his training. Please do not think that these remarks portend a jeremiad. " Are we downhearted? No! " I need only present to you an analysis of the statistics given on pages 20 and 21 of Professor Fiske's Report covering the examinations of June, 1918. The ordinary examinations in seventeen different subjects were taken by 9,889 candidates with the following result for the first eight places:

Subject	Number of Candidates	60–100 Percent
1. Greek	698	67.5
2. Mathematics	11,646	62.9
3. Latin	8,314	59.9
4. Botany	58	58.6
5. French	4,664	58.0
6. Physics	1,829	52.9
7. Chemistry	992	52.2
8. Zoölogy	14	50.0

In these seventeen subjects the Board held fifty separate examinations, e.g., Mathematics A2, Latin 3, French A. If we consider examinations that were taken by at least ninety-nine candidates (one percent of the total number), we shall find that in twenty-two of the fifty, more than one-half of the candidates secured 60 percent or higher. If we arrange these twenty-two separate examinations in the order of their superiority, as Professor C. H. Forbes did at the close of his admirable paper on " The Sham Argument against Latin," we shall note with satisfaction the following result: Greek BG, Greek CH, Mathematics A2, Mathematics A, Latin 3, Mathematics B, Latin 4, Latin 5, French A, Latin 6, Mathematics D, Greek A2, Latin 2, Mathematics F, Mathematics C, Latin 1, 2, 4, English 1, French B, Physics, Chemistry, Greek A1, German A. In other words, of the first five places, Greek has two, Mathematics two, Latin one; of the first ten places, Latin has four, Mathematics three, Greek two, French one; of the first fifteen places, Mathematics has six, Latin five, Greek three, French one. Only one of the Latin examinations taken by any considerable number of candidates failed to secure a place among these twenty-two, viz., Latin 1, Grammar, in which, alas, only 43.9 percent out of 1,024 candidates secured 60 percent or higher. We may, however, console ourselves by the fact that Latin 3, Second-Year Latin, involving translation at sight only, with relevant questions on grammar and composition, stood fifth in the entire list of fifty examinations and only 28.9 percent of 1,901 candidates failed to secure 60 percent or higher. It is, then, beyond cavil that, so far as the statistics of the Board for 1918, covering the performance of nearly 10,000 individual pupils, throw light upon the results of secondary education, Mathematics, Latin, and Greek are easily the best taught subjects in the United States.

Can we do better? I think we can and should. We can and should in the translation of every Latin sentence in the classroom throughout the entire course call into play as our most potent helper that general intelligence, that mother wit, the possession and use of which distinguishes a human being from a parrot. With mother wit on the alert, *ex pede Herculem* becomes possible; without mother wit, even a very fair amount of information about syntax may lead to an incorrect translation. A knowledge of vocabulary is in general absolutely indispensable, but even here intelligence can in not a few cases make good a temporary deficiency, not by any haphazard guess, but through the logical compulsion of the words that are known. Why should we fear to train as at least a by-product of our work something that is akin to the scientific imagination? Some scientists claim that " the development and discipline of the imagination is the best gift of science to our intellectual life, and hence to liberal education." [8]

Let me make my meaning clear by a few sentences taken from First-Year Latin books, with some *variae lectiones* of my own. I shall assume an intelligent pupil who knows the meanings of the Latin words, who has a decent knowledge of the forms and their simple meanings as given with the paradigms, but whose acquaintance with case and mood constructions is extremely limited. With this relatively slender equipment he relies as much as possible upon his mother wit; but, having come to regard his teacher as a sensible person, he obeys the three commandments that have been declared to be necessary to salvation: (1) Rely upon the order of the Latin words as a sure clue to the meaning of the sentence; (2) Never identify a Latin word with one single English word, for words are at best only symbols and the English rendering [9] should vary according to the context; (3) Distrust every apparent meaning of a sentence which does not agree with ordinary common sense.

[8] See Professor E. B. Wilson's noble address, " Science and Liberal Education," *Science*, XLII (Nov. 5, 1915), pp. 625–30.

[9] See H. C. Nutting, " The Translation of Latin," *The Classical Journal*, V (1910), pp. 165–70. Professor Nutting gives an interesting list of fifteen different renderings of *magnus*.

Listen to such a pupil as he comments on some Latin sentences. *Aquam nautae amant.* Only one meaning possible. *Vitam nautae amant:* " Sailors love life." Perhaps; but so do other people. Why then say so? " They love a sailor's life." Much more sensible, and therefore more likely. But I cannot be sure until I know what circumstances called forth the remark. *Decem annis Caesar multa bella gessit:* " For (during) ten years Caesar waged many wars." Possibly, but he must have had his hands full in fighting many different foes at once. " In (within) ten years Caesar waged many wars." Much more sensible, and therefore more likely. *Decem annis Caesar duo milia hominum interfecit.* Only one meaning possible, viz., " In (within) ten years . . ." *Urbem defensoribus vacuam reppererunt.* Let us suppose for a moment that he ignores the forms almost absolutely. He writes down the English equivalents of the Latin words in their order: " city defenders empty have found." Do these words mean " The defenders found the city empty "? Unlikely. One would expect the assailants, not the defenders, to find the city empty. " The city found the defenders empty "? Nonsense! Intelligence is thus forced to a correct translation with almost no help from the forms. *Avari milites aras spoliaverunt donis:* " Greedy soldiers altars have despoiled gifts." Every combination nonsensical except one. Again a correct translation with almost no help from forms. *Ipsius Sullae domum deleverunt, filios et uxorem fuga salutem petere coegerunt:* " Himself Sulla home they destroyed, sons and wife flight safety to seek they compelled." One bit of syntax is here requisite, viz., the case of home, for it might be *at home.* This determined, every combination, as before, is nonsensical save the right one. *Omnibus rebus ad profectionem comparatis diem constituunt qua die ad ripam Rhodani omnes conveniant:* " all things to (for) departure procured day they fix which day to bank Rhone all they assemble." As *comparatis* obviously goes with *rebus,* this collocation leads to an inevitable result except for one momentary doubt. Do they all *actually* assemble? Then why not Indicative Mood? Ah! one naturally fixes a day for a meeting, a day on which to meet. " They fix, then, a day on which they are all to assemble at the bank of the Rhone." Quite sensible!

Consider now parts of two sentences from the passage set last June for translation at sight on Latin 5.

. . . fluctibus actos
atra subegit hiems vestris succedere terris

" waves driven black has forced winter (storm) your to approach lands." Evidently X (identity not yet clear) " has forced " Y (identity not yet clear) " to approach your lands." What next? What further slight acquaintance with grammar will yet suffice? Simply this, that *actos* is accusative plural, while *fluctibus* is not, *subegit* is singular, and *atra* and *hiems* are both nominative. Only one translation is now reasonable.

Sive fide seu quis bello est expertus et armis

" Whether good faith or anyone war has tested and arms." " Whether . . . or " gives a choice between two different things. " Good faith " then is clearly different from " war and arms," and must express some friendly relation. The words then yield apparently perfectly good sense: " Whether anyone has tested good faith or war and arms." But the nouns because of their forms cannot be the objects of the verb, and one commonly makes a

test " by " some means or " in " some way. The object
of the verb must now be sought in the main clause, and
is clearly the idea expressed in the preceding verse in
the words *dextram potentem.* Our pupil, however, will
perhaps be content with the following translation:
" Whether anyone has made a test in friendship or in
war and arms." The correct translation is thus forced
with only slight help from syntax; yet both these sentences, especially the second, caused great difficulty last
June to fourth-year candidates.

Latin abounds in whole sentences or whole clauses
whose meaning can be determined by the exercise of intelligence in the manner that I have roughly sketched.
Shall we, then, eliminate the study of syntax? *Di meliora
duint!* But it is certainly tragic if information about
syntax, instead of helping intelligence to operate more
swiftly and more confidently actually confuses it, or even
tends to its disuse. A fully inflected language like Latin
provides constant guideposts to the meaning such as
are lacking in a comparatively uninflected language like
English. I beg your consideration of a number of English
passages for whose meaning the reader is forced to rely
wholly upon mother wit. With the exception of some
from Milton's *Paradise Lost* these passages are all taken
from books in the lists upon which the Board's entrance
examinations in English are based. On the paper in English 2 — Literature, for last June you will find a passage
of seventeen verses from Book I of *Paradise Lost* which
opens as follows:

> Darkened so, yet shone
> Above them all the Archangel: but his face
> Deep scars of thunder had intrenched, and care
> Sat on his faded cheek.

Is " face " the subject or the object of " had intrenched "?
There are only two possibilities, and there is for an intelligent pupil only one sensible answer. If such a pupil should read further in Book I he would of course find no difficulty in

> Him the Almighty Power
> Hurled headlong flaming from the ethereal sky.

English here gives at the outset the help of inflection that is characteristic of Latin. But presently he would meet

> There the companions of his fall, o'erwhelmed
> With floods and whirlwinds of tempestuous fire,
> He soon discerns.

Until our pupil reaches the third verse, he cannot be sure of the construction of " companions," for clearly Milton might have written " Him soon discern."

> That glory never shall his wrath or might
> Extort from me.

> The roof was fretted gold. Not Babilon
> Nor great Alcairo such magnificence
> Equalled in all their glories.

The context makes the meaning clear in much the same way as it does for the verse

> nec Troiam Ausonios gremio excepisse pigebit.

In spite of the logic of the facts, aided by the caption of the sight passage, this verse troubled the candidates in Vergil last June.

> or faery elves,
> Whose midnight revels, by a forest-side
> Or fountain, some belated peasant sees.

In the last passage the verb " sees," when it comes, makes the connection between " revels " and " peasant " perfectly clear. If, instead of " sees," Milton had written "charm" or "fright," the relation between the two nouns would have been reversed, but this relation would have been understood with equal ease from the nature of the ideas alone.

But let us now turn to the books in the English list:

> "It is the last time — 'tis the last,"
> He muttered thrice, — "the last time e'er
> That angel voice shall Roderick hear." [10]

Write "cheer" for "hear" and note the result of the change.

> From Chillon's snow-white battlement
> Which round about the wave inthrals. [11]

But change "wave" to "doomed" or "lost."

> Hands, that the rod of Empire might have swayed. [12]

But Gray could have said, "Hearts, that the joys of Empire might have swayed." Note now a few verses that might cause a moment's, but only a moment's, hesitation.

> Now in the Castle-park drew out
> Their chequered bands the joyous rout. [13]

> Gently he dried the falling tear
> And gently whispered hope and cheer.
> Her faltering steps, half led, half staid,
> Through gallery fair and high arcade
> Till at his touch, its wings of pride
> A portal arch unfolded wide. [14]

> A blither heart, till Ellen came,
> Did never love nor sorrow tame. [15]

> And all the air a solemn stillness holds. [16]

---

[10] *The Lady of the Lake*, Canto III, sec. xxx.
[11] *The Prisoner of Chillon.*
[12] *Elegy Written in a Country Churchyard.*
[13] *The Lady of the Lake*, Canto V, sec. xxii.
[14] *Ibid.*, Canto VI, sec. xxv.
[15] *Ibid.*, Canto II, sec. xxv.
[16] *Elegy Written in a Country Churchyard.*

Whose turf, whose shade, whose flowers among
Wanders the hoary Thames along
   His silver-winding way.[17]

Prancing in pride of earthly trust,
His charger hurled him to the dust,
And, by a base plebeian thrust,
He died his band before.[18]

While the cock, with lively din,
Scatters the rear of darkness thin,
And to the stack, or the barn-door,
Stoutly struts his dames before.[19]

Observe that in the last three passages the prepositions " among " and " before " follow the nouns that they govern. Why in the sight passage on Latin 5 last June should

Fata per Aeneae iuro dextramque potentem

cause more than momentary hesitation?

The Chief in silence strode before.[20]

Suppose that the poet of the *L'Allegro* passage had been a feminist, and had written the last verse thus:

Stoutly strut his dames before.

Ability to distinguish a verb in the plural from a verb in the singular is all that is needed to understand at once the altered picture. The change in the function of the word " before " causes no difficulty at all.

Can a pupil, if intelligent, see in advance as he reads a sentence the idea, though not necessarily the exact words, with which that sentence must reasonably close? Yes, in not a few cases.

---

[17] *On a Distant Prospect of Eton College.*
[18] *Marmion,* Canto V, sec. xxxi.
[19] *L'Allegro.*
[20] *Lady of the Lake,* Canto V, sec. xii.

Th' applause of list'ning senates to command,
The threats of pain and ruin to despise,
To scatter plenty o'er a smiling land,
And read their history in a nation's eyes,

Their lot forbad. . . .[21]

The last three words might have been different, but not the general idea. For eight stanzas Gray has been describing "their destiny obscure." The close of the following is in like fashion inevitable.

. . . Yet not the more
Cease I to wander where the Muses haunt
Clear spring, or shady grove, or sunny hill,
Smit with the love of sacred song; but chief
Thee, Sion, and the flowery brooks beneath,
That wash thy hallowed feet, and warbling flow,
Nightly I visit. . . .[22]

Read the third and fourth stanzas of *Lycidas* and see how confidently one may predict the verse

Fanning their joyous leaves to thy soft lays.

Let us return to the Latin. As one reads the opening paragraph of the first speech against Catiline and declaims to himself the fourth sentence with its six times repeated *nihil*, is he not sure, long before he reaches it, of the general idea of the verb with which the indignant question must close? *Patere tua consilia non sentis? Constrictam iam.* . . . The reader knows full well what is coming. "We've got you, Catiline, because we know everything (*patere tua consilia* is repeated in *horum omnium scientia*); don't you see it?" (How much do we know?) *Quid proxima, quid superiore nocte egeris, ubi fueris, quos convocaveris, quid consili ceperis* — How will the speaker end? Inevitably with the idea, in

[21] *Elegy Written in a Country Churchyard.*
[22] *Paradise Lost* iii. 26–32.

whatever words it may be expressed, of *horum omnium scientia*, " we all know." Both sentences, like the five that precede, are cast in the interrogative form, and this, too, is practically inevitable.

Let me add two further instances from the paper in Latin 4 last June. *Quo igitur animo esse existimatis aut eos qui vectigalia nobis pensitant aut eos qui . . .* In the detailed argument which Cicero has for some time been making about the *vectigalia,* what two classes are most likely to be thus bracketed together? Surely those who have to pay and those who must collect in order not to lose money by their contract with the State. *Itaque, credo, si civis Romanus Archias legibus non esset.* The rest of this sentence, *ut ab aliquo imperatore civitate donaretur, perficere potuit* is practically inevitable, for Cicero has just told the jury that Pompey gave citizenship to Theophanes, *scriptorem rerum suarum.*

In these two sentences, as in hundreds of others, the course of Cicero's thought is so sequent that an alert intelligence cannot well lose the scent. The path, too, is well marked. The principle of balance is almost everywhere observable. This aspect of his style is so familiar to you all that I need not here enlarge upon it. I have recently read the whole of the speech *Pro Lege Manilia* with sole reference to this symmetrical grouping of facts and ideas, and I am convinced that Cicero has used it almost to excess. The path is often very simply marked, e.g., by *et . . . et, neque . . . neque, non solum . . . sed etiam, non tam . . . quam, non . . . sed, maiores nostri . . . vos,* or by connectives standing at or near the beginning of the sentence, *quae res, tamen, igitur, cum vero;* but the signboards are perhaps too numerous and too clear. One thinks at times, regretfully, of the pleasures of an intellectual cross-country tramp where one might now and then get lost, and be forced to use one's wits quite carefully in order not to stay lost.

As I pointed out in the early part of this paper, the tests used in the army were devised to discover, together with other things, a man's ability " to analyze a situation and to maintain a state of mental alertness." It is obviously a new and unexpected situation that gives intelligence its opportunity. In war, as in ordinary life, intelligence is most conspicuously shown " under fire." It has been a matter of some pride that since 1911 the question papers in Latin showed no misprint. We were sore distressed, therefore, last June at the mistake in the numbering of the verses of the first passage for translation on Latin 5, Virgil. Let me say here in passing that the examiners recovered their peace of mind when they found that the final proof on file in Professor Fiske's office showed both numbers (95–100) in their correct position at the side of the passage. But of this the candidates were unaware. How then did they meet the unexpected and disturbing situation? The numbers at the right-hand side indicated verses 93–102, the numbers at the end verses 92–101. " Mental alertness " was needed to discover which numbering was correct. Four of the questions involved specific Latin words, after each of which was placed in parentheses the number of the verse in which it stood. These four numbers all agreed with the numbers given at the end of the passage, viz., 92–101. If the numbers at the side were right, there were six misprints, four of them in four separate questions. If, however, these numbers were right, the two numbers at the side were misplaced. I submit that the " mental alertness," desiderated by the army tests, should have " ana-

lyzed the situation " correctly. But " mental alertness "
seems to be put to flight by the artillery of examinations.
Of course, no candidate was allowed to suffer because of
the dislocation of the side numbers.

One question upon the paper in Cicero deserves some
special comment. " Describe the method of collecting the
vectigalia of the province of Asia; and explain in this
connection why *familiae* were kept *in saltibus, in agris,*
and *in portubus atque custodiis.*" You will recall that
Cicero devotes sections 14–19 (two and one-half pages
out of thirty, Oxford text), inclusive, to a detailed discussion of the stability of the Roman financial system as
affected by the war. He has already (in sections 14 and
15) said: *Asia vero tam opima est ac fertilis ut et ubertate*
agrorum et varietate fructuum et magnitudine pastionis
et multitudine earum rerum quae exportentur facile
omnibus terris antecellat. . . . Nam cum hostium
copiae non longe absunt, etiam si inruptio nulla facta est,
tamen pecuaria relinquitur, agri cultura deseritur, mer-
catorum navigatio conquiescit. Ita neque ex portu neque
ex decumis neque ex scriptura vectigalia conservari po-
test. He has thus already three times explicitly described
the three sources of revenue that in the passage set last
June for translation he again describes for the fourth
time by the phrases *in saltibus, in agris,* and *in portubus*
atque custodiis. The candidate has just defined in his
translation the two classes that are endangered by the
war, *aut eos qui vectigalia nobis pensitant aut eos qui*
exercent atque exigunt. I have just examined again the
notes on these sections of ten school editions of Cicero's
Orations, including, I think, all that are widely used. All
ten editions give clear and definite notes upon the three
kinds of taxes, eight of the ten state that the *familiae*

were the agents or assistants of the *publicani* in collecting
these taxes, and seven of the ten distinguish by translation into English *exercent* from *exigunt,* adding that the
first word refers to the *publicani* who make the contracts
with the state, and the second to their agents who actually collect the money. Like so many other questions
that appear upon these papers, this question that I am
now discussing sought to ascertain whether the candidate was dealing in his translation with words, or with
facts and ideas. A correct answer involved nothing beyond a reasonable understanding of the concrete meaning for Roman life of the words which he had just translated. The question was poorly answered, and revealed
striking ignorance of the relation of the *publicani* to the
state and to the tax-payer, of the function of the *familiae*
as the fiscal agents of the *publicani,* and of the three
sources of revenue which, as I have reminded you, Cicero
specifically describes four times within the limits of a
single page of the Oxford text. The *publicani* were not
interested in landscape. They kept their *familiae* in three
kinds of places for professional reasons, and if they had
agents in each place, it was because each place had necessarily its own business significance.

Let me give you one example of an unintelligent answer: " The families were kept in marshes, fields, and
safe places so that they could escape these wicked tax-
collectors, and also to evade the armies of Mithridates
and Tigranes."

Sulla's activities as a salesman were remarkable. One
of the readers collected the following list:

" Sulla was selling — offices in the province — sou-
venirs for the benefit of the soldiers — citizenships —
works of poets — possessions of a man who had run into

debt — rewards to the people — assignments to the different provinces — patents to the Romans — public offices — centurionships — many copies of the writing of the poets. Sulla was exchanging money of the different foreign nations. Sulla had at one time been a sort of peddlar (*sic*). Sulla demanded tribute of him, saying that he had no right to go there and sell his verses for so much money because he was not a Roman citizen. Sulla bought all the books which he had on his stand. Sulla was praetor and therefore auctioneer. Sulla allowed the poems of the wicked to be sold in the public places of the city."

One of the readers made the following list of the *duo reges:* " Mithrades, Mithridates king of Syria, Tiranes, Tyghrenes, Tigranes king of Tigranocerta, Tigranes and his son-in-law Mithradates, Ariobarzanes, Arizzobanes, Antiochus III, Pompey, Lucullus, Crassus, Murena, Julius Caesar and Augustus Caesar, Marius, Sulla, Sertorius, Jugurtha, Spartacus, Ariovistus, Pyrrhus, Archimedes, Cyrus, Artaxerxes, Datis, Alexander, Attila, Nicomedes, Appius, Agamemnon, Astyanax, Pontus, Numidicus, Cyxicus, Regius, Arzontheus, Andramitus, Siaticus."

Listen now to two good answers.

"*Fato:* Death by fate would be a natural death, in which she had no power at all. If the gods decreed that she should die, it would be death by fate. There were three Fates or *Parcae* — one which held the distaff, one which spun the thread of life, and one which cut it off. *Merita morte:* refers to death that may or may not have been planned by the Fates. Had Dido done anything contrary or displeasing to the will of the gods, she would have merited death even though the Fates had not thus decreed it for her. The *merita morte* depends more directly on the will of the gods and on her manner of life."

" From the passage assigned we gain the idea that Aeneas was not afraid of death. He envied those who had been able to die gloriously. He thought that those men who had died there were much better off than he, who had lived. The idea expressed by Vergil is precisely that of Coningsby Dawson in *Carry On,* namely, the man who dies in a glorious cause on a battlefield dies in a moment of elevation of character at the height of his career. As Dawson says, Aeneas' idea was ' It doesn't matter when or where you die, but how and for what cause.' "

In this last answer, with its impromptu correlation of ancient and modern feeling, that intelligence which is the subject of this paper is seen actively at work. Let us commend it, in all the forms in which it may display itself, to the fostering care of every teacher of Latin, and let us so commend it by our practice as well as by precept. Let us combine " information and training," grammar and intelligence. But let us never forget that the object of all education is " to render an intelligent being yet more intelligent." The acquisition of information is a means to this end. Except, perhaps, in the education of slaves, it is not an end in itself.

TRAINING VERSUS EDUCATION[1]

FOR SOME WEEKS as I have entered or left the building
in which I have my office I have had occasion to note on
the bulletin board the announcement of a Student Con-
ference to be held at South Orange, New Jersey. The legend runs: " A Changing World and a Static Church?
Has the Church's Program Kept Pace with the World's
Needs? " The words have led my mind afield. I have re-
called the remark made by Cicero in the first book of his
*Tusculans: magni autem est ingeni sevocare mentem
a sensibus et cogitationem ab consuetudine abducere.*
Cicero, you will remember, is speaking of those early inquirers who were the first to conceive of a life of the soul
quite independent of that of the body and therefore capable of continued existence after the dissolution of the
body. We may associate with such a display of imaginative power the vision of that thinker, presumably earlier
than Leucippus, who saw in the piece of wood or stone before him, to his senses absolutely motionless, the ever-
lasting dance of the atoms. The vogue of the moving picture today reminds us that at all times the eye has played
a larger part in the formation of ideas than the brain. The
senses, whose evidence has again and again been proved
untrustworthy, still rule in the thinking processes of the
great majority of mankind. Nor is this wonderful. Often-
times, as I have stood upon some height which, like the
crest of the Shawungunk Range, commands a wide plain,

[1] A paper read at the fifteenth annual meeting of the Classical Association
of New England, at Wesleyan University, April 3, 1920. Reprinted from *The
Classical Journal,* May, 1920.

I have noted how natural it was for the untraveled man
to feel as a matter of course that the earth was flat. We
tend instinctively to become creatures of our environment, creatures of habit, conservative in thought and action. Only varied experience and repeated discovery that
the world is somewhat larger than is suggested by our
own individual lives will in the end make us independent
of *consuetudo,* use and wont. In an age in which the mu-
tability of ideas and institutions is brought home to us
every day, in which principles are bluntly challenged that
to many of us have seemed axiomatic, in which proposals
are enthusiastically, and often heatedly, urged for instant adoption that seem to some minds suitable material
for supplementary chapters to *Alice in Wonderland,* I
turn to save my peace of mind to the picture which anthropology has gradually drawn for us of the history of
mankind from those far-distant ages when as yet man
had neither language nor fire down to the wonders of
our own times. I have been reading recently Professor
Breasted's fascinating presentation of *Ancient Times.*
The pageant of man in history, of his slow advance,
incredibly slow at first, during the thousands and
thousands of years that preceded the dawn of historic
civilization, followed by the wonderful efflorescence and
kaleidoscopic change of his life in the Orient, in Egypt, in
Greece, and in the far-flung dominion of Rome — even
this section of universal history presents to us a series of
events of the most diversified character in which the principle of metamorphosis is continually at work. But this,
as I have said, is but a section of universal history, for the
book closes with the coronation of Charlemagne in A.D.
800. Let us add now in our imagination the changes in society and government, in the arts of life, and in ideas and

ideals in every field of thought that have marked the
history of the world since Charlemagne. Are we not
forced to admit that, as Heraclitus says, πάντα ῥεῖ, *omnia
fluunt?* Change is indeed the diet on which all subsist
and, I cannot but believe, is seen to be the hallmark of
life. Individual men or groups of men may fear it; but
their attitude is irrelevant, for history shows that there is
no permanence. We may guide, at least to some extent,
the forces of change, but we cannot prevent their activity.
Their vitality lies at the very heart of the world.

One specious aspect of permanence may for a moment
deceive us. Certain words expressive of ideas and systems
reappear again and again during the centuries and millennia; but, if we examine these recurrences in a Socratic
fashion, we readily discover that the meanings of these
words do not really remain the same. The term " elec-
toral college," for example, no longer connotes the same
kind of political action that it did in the early days of our
Republic. If, then, change is the universal law, the principle of it should, or rather must, enter into our voluntary
intellectual and spiritual life. Since in some fashion or
other it will come, whether we welcome or fear it, the part
of wisdom is to guide the stream. And we are particularly
compelled to consider what practical sagacity would ad-
vise us to do when we are facing, as we are today, most
serious problems of reconstruction. It is already exceedingly doubtful whether the world may reasonably hope
to solve these problems if it approaches them in the same
frame of mind in which it attempted their solution prior
to August 1, 1914. Each of us must cheerfully admit as
prerequisite to effective action the truth of Hamlet's
remark:

> There are more things in heaven and earth, Horatio,
> Than are dreamt of in your philosophy.

We teachers are fond of commenting upon the meaning of the word " education." We *seem* at least to be aware of the implication in the elements of its formation. Are we really anxious to educate? Or do we wish rather to train? For we may note that, while all education necessarily involves training, there may easily be training which is not, in the proper sense of the word, education, and we must further remember that, if we educate our pupils in the arts of self-expression, their views, judged by our own standards, will often seem rather heterodox. There is as yet no way known to the world in which minds, whether young or old, may be at once granted liberty of thought and refused permission to think incorrectly. Such is the diversity of human nature that, if we really succeed in the classroom in persuading a vigorous mind to take delight in the exercise of its powers, we shall probably at times be unable to prevent the adoption of views of which we ourselves cannot approve. For myself, I hold with Emerson [2] that

Nature, when she sends a new mind into the world, fills it beforehand with the desire for that which she wishes it to know and do. Let us wait and see what is this new creation, of what new organ the great Spirit had need when it incarnated this new will. . . . The charm of life is this variety of genius, these contrasts and flavors by which Heaven has modulated the identity of truth, and there is a perpetual hankering to violate this individuality, to warp his ways of thinking and behaviour to resemble or reflect your thinking and behaviour. A low self-love in the parent desires that his child should repeat his character and fortune; an expectation which the child, if justice is done him, will nobly disappoint. By working on the theory that this resemblance exists, we shall do what in us lies to defeat his proper promise and produce the ordinary and mediocre.

May I at this point recall to your minds a bit of modern Latin that has become almost proverbial:

[2] " Education," p. 12.

Tempora mutantur, nos et mutamur in illis.

The first half of this observation is undoubtedly true; may we say the same of the second half? The criticism of the traditional scope and methods of the teaching of mathematics in high school and college has led to a coöperative investigation involving almost all the mathematical teachers in the country. There is already substantial certainty of a notable readjustment of the presentation of this subject to the needs of today. I should like to urge the desirability of a similar coöperative investigation to be conducted by Latinists in the interest of the future of Latin.

May I say again, as I have said on many previous occasions, that personally I have long been confident that all literature should be taught as a form of dramatic action. If, now, we wish to make our pupils sensitive to the dramatic quality which is implicit in all that has come down to us from the great Latin writers, we shall find that the order in which the Latin words are arranged in the sentence is our most helpful instrument. In every well-constructed Latin sentence the march of the words or more often of the word groups (for the word groups are really the blocks out of which the sentence is built) represents normally the gradual emergence of the idea into shape. The march of the syntax does not necessarily or even usually coincide with the march of the ideas. If you are familiar with the illuminating essay of Professor Henri Weil, entitled in the English translation *The Order of Words in the Ancient Languages Compared with the Modern Languages,* you will perhaps recall the passage [3] in which the great French scholar makes this clear:

[3] Henri Weil, *De l'ordre des mots dans les langues anciennes comparées aux langues modernes* (Paris, 1844). English translation, with notes and additions by

The fact that Romulus founded the city of Rome can, in languages that admit of free construction, be stated in several different ways, preserving all the time the same syntax. Suppose that some one has related the story of the birth of Romulus and the marvellous events that attach thereto, he might add *idem Romulus Romam condidit* [to the same Romulus Rome owes its foundation]. While showing a traveler the city of Rome, we might say to him *hanc urbem condidit Romulus* [this city was founded by Romulus]. Speaking of the most celebrated foundings, and after mentioning the founding of Thebes by Cadmus, that of Athens by Cecrops, we might add *condidit Romam Romulus* [the foundation of Rome was due to Romulus]. The syntax is the same in the three sentences; in all three the subject is *Romulus,* the attribute *founded,* the direct object *Rome.* Nevertheless, three different things are said in the three sentences because these elements, though remaining the same, are distributed in a different manner in the introduction and the principal part of the sentence. The point of departure, the rallying point of the interlocutors, is Romulus the first time, Rome the second, and the third time the idea of founding. And so the information that is to be imparted to another, the goal of the discourse, is different in the three forms of expression.

In the principle governing the determination of the word order which Professor Weil has thus stated we have in effect the principle that governs the moving picture. Each new idea comes out of that which has preceded it and leads in turn to that which follows. A good translator will therefore endeavor to find such forms of expression as will enable him to retain in the translation the order of the words which is found in the original. Do you remember the amusing fashion in which in the *Pickwick Papers* Dickens makes Alfred Jingle express his thoughts.

Ah! you should keep dogs — fine animals — sagacious creatures — dog of my own once — pointer — surprising instinct — out shooting one day — entering enclosure — whistled — dog stopped — whistled again — Ponto — no go; stock still — called him —

Charles W. Super (Boston, 1877), pp. 29, 30. The translations of the Latin sentences included in the quotation are not in the original, but have been added by the present writer, following the order of the Latin words.

Ponto — Ponto — wouldn't move — dog transfixed — staring at a board — looked up, saw an inscription — " Gamekeeper has orders to shoot all dogs found in this enclosure " — wouldn't pass it — wonderful dog — valuable dog, that — very.

Obviously, we have here no closely woven web of thought. Each new element in the picture stands by itself and the mind is asked to supply the necessary connecting threads. Let us take a hint then from Mr. Jingle in order to represent with some degree of success in English words the effect of the order in which the Latin words are purposely arranged by the writer. I venture to use for this purpose a short but very graphic description for which we have to thank the unknown author of *De Bello Africo*. It was used last June on the Comprehensive paper in Latin. My translation will of course be quite free.

Non videtur esse praetermittendum it does not seem right to pass over in silence *de virtute cuiusdam veterani* the bravery of a certain veteran. *Nam cum in sinistro cornu* the scene is the left wing *elephans* here is an elephant *vulneratus et dolore concitatus* he is wounded and the pain has maddened him *in hominem* we see a man *inermem* he has no weapon *impetum fecisset* the elephant makes a rush at him *deinde eum sub pedem subiectum* he is under the elephant's foot *genu innixus* the elephant kneels on him *pondere suo* with all its weight *proboscide erecta vibrantique* the trunk is high in the air and quivering *premeret atque necaret* the pressure is killing the man, *veteranus* here is the veteran *hic non potuit pati* he cannot endure the situation *quin se armatus bestiae offerret* he has a weapon, the animal must be stopped. *Quem postquam elephans ad se telo venire animadvertit* the elephant becomes aware of the approach of the soldier with a weapon *relicto homine* it abandons the man *militem* he turns to the soldier *proboscide circumdat* its trunk is flung around him *atque in sublime extollit* and up into the air the soldier goes. *Armatus* we note again the presence of a weapon *qui in eiusmodi periculo* the danger is acute *constanter agendum sibi videret* resolution was necessary, it was clear *gladio* out comes the sword *proboscidem caedere* the trunk is cut open *quantum viribus poterat* the soldier uses all his strength *non destitit* he does not stop. *Quo dolore adductus* the pain has its effect *ele-*

phans milite abiecto the elephant throws the soldier down *maximo cum stridore* it trumpets loudly *conversus* it turns *ad reliquas bestias se recepit* to the rest of the animals it makes its way.

The translation which I have just given you has been built up by adding one detail to another in such a way that the dramatic function of each new element was noted by the mind before the next element followed it. This, as I said before, is the principle of the moving picture, and evidently, as I also said before, the march of the syntax is not the march of the ideas. In every story, however, it is the ideas that count with the hearer and not the mechanism of the grammar. If in any bit of graphic description, such, for example, as is mentioned above, you are careful to let the picture form itself in your mind step by step, as the successive important word or word groups are apprehended by both eye and ear, you will, I am sure, be convinced that the Latin word order is admirably adapted to the purposes of vivid narration. The freedom of the arrangement of words makes it possible for the writer to conceive his picture in any way that he chooses; and, broadly speaking, the order in which the words or word groups stand is the order in which he wishes his story to take shape in the mind of the reader. Let me translate to you, in similar fashion, two more simple instances, this time from the third speech against Catiline. Cicero is describing the arrest of the Gallic envoys at the Mulvian bridge.

Interim meanwhile *tertia fere vigilia exacta* the night was almost three-quarters over *cum iam pontem* here is the bridge *magno comitatu* look at the size of the crowd *legati Allobrogum* we see the envoys of the Allobroges *ingredi inciperent* they step upon the bridge *unaque Volturcius* Ah! there is Volturcius with them *fit in eos impetus* the officers rush at them *educuntur et ab illis gladii* out come their swords *et a nostris* and ours too.

In this description, the last two clauses are naturally opened by the verbs *fit* and *educuntur;* for everything is happening very rapidly. In the last clause the *et* which precedes *ab illis* makes it at once almost certain that another *et* will follow to introduce a balancing phrase for *ab illis.*

The second passage closely follows the first in Cicero's story.

Atque interea and meantime *statim* no time is lost *admonitu Allobrogum* the hint comes from the Allobroges *C. Sulpicium praetorem* here's Sulpicius, the praetor *fortem virum* he is a determined man *misi* I sent him *qui ex aedibus Cethegi* the house of Cethegus is involved *si quid telorum esset* if any weapons were there *efferret* he was to bring them out *ex quibus ille maximum sicarum numerum* he found a lot of daggers *et gladiorum* and of swords too *extulit* he brought them out.

In the passages which I have chosen, as in scores of others, the order of the words corresponds to the march of the ideas but not necessarily to the march of the syntax. Consider now a sentence from the earlier part of the same speech against Catiline in which the clash between these two orders is, I think, intentional:

Principio ut Catilina paucis ante diebus erupit ex urbe, cum sceleris sui socios, huiusce nefarii belli acerrimos duces, Romae reliquisset, semper vigilavi et providi, Quirites, quem ad modum in tantis et tam absconditis insidiis salvi esse possemus.

In this sentence the ideas expressed in the first two clauses are antithetical. Catiline is gone from the city, his accomplices are still at Rome. If Cicero had made the march of the syntax identical with the march of the ideas, the nominative *socii* would have been used instead of the accusative *socios,* and the verb *relinquere* would have been used in the passive voice, or would perhaps have been replaced by *manerent.* The use of the active voice and the accusative case is almost certainly due to the desire to keep Catiline the subject of the second verb as he is inevitably the subject of the first. The principle involved is wholly dramatic, Catiline still occupies the center of the stage and deliberately leaves behind him at Rome the men whom Cicero, a moment later, describes as *maximo furore et scelere inflammatos*. Upon this principle, as well as upon the principle that, as we have seen, governs in general the order of the words in Latin we may properly make this comment. In the external world we gain our information through the senses, and hosts of sensations have become automatic because of countless repetition. Whenever words can be so used and so arranged that, if we understand their meaning, they have upon us as nearly as possible the same effect that the objects or actions themselves would instantly have produced upon us, a great step has been taken toward lucidity.

To prevent misunderstanding let me frankly admit that the operation of the principle for which I am contending is not so clearly observable in all Latin sentences, even in prose, as in those which I have cited. Its presence is easiest to trace in descriptions of rapid action in the external world. I have myself found some difficulty in applying this principle to the word order of expositions of mental processes. In poetry, especially in hexameter verse, its activity is seriously affected by the exigencies of quantity, and by the development of certain forms of balance in the relation of nouns and adjectives that are highly artificial even if artistic. Subject, however, to these limitations, and to some further details which Professor Weil discusses, the principle appears to me to be sound and of very great importance. It is quite pertinent to the idea expressed in the title of my paper. A pupil who learns to make in this way the preliminary translation that he subsequently molds into fluent English will find it, I think, impossible to do his work in any merely mechanical fashion. This method cannot be reduced to a rule. It is the nemesis of rules that they enable the user to dispense with thinking. The mind that is merely well trained need not at the moment think at all. In fact the perfection of training, in the sense in which I am distinguishing the word from education, is attained when the mind operates with the accuracy and speed of a steel machine, and with as little thought. Our current methods of translating have, I fear, become so stereotyped and are so closely associated with formal rules of grammar that the absurd versions with which we are so familiar do not seem to ruffle at all the peace of mind of our protégés. They can write, for example, " of these two men, each was stronger than the other " and feel the satisfaction that comes from a duty properly performed. Last June the readers in Cicero were informed that " already in truth the soldiers hibernate daily, sermons and letters are preferred "; that " not only is so great a band of the army said to have been killed but not any particle of anyone has been found." One candidate explained the distinction between *manus* and *vestigium* by saying that " *manus* refers to those troops directly under Pompey's command; the *vestigium*, however, was scattered about and it was much harder to control their actions." Let me say in passing that I have examined the notes on this passage of Cicero in thirteen school editions. In eleven of the thirteen a full explanation of Cicero's meaning is given, and in the remaining two at least some help. This cheerful slumber of the mind appears also in the use of general terms. Many candidates told us quite correctly that *scilicet* in the passage set from the *Pro Archia* gave the tone of "irony" or "sarcasm," but these same candidates in their translation rendered the word variously as follows: "it is sought for," "it is permitted," "let it be," "it is agreed." In this same passage the verb *esse censam* was so often translated "censored" or "censured" or "censered" that, if the readers had been influenced by the psychology of advertising, they would have discarded their previous ideas about this verb in favor of the new renderings. The Bible evidently is still read, for we learned that "Creusa became a stone image because she looked back after the family had left Troy." And Venus was not unaware of the complexity of family life when she said to Aeneas: "No longer you perceive where Anchises lingers by his old parents, suppressed by his wife, Creusa, by his son Ascanius."

The second passage set for translation on the Vergil paper closed with the verses:

Litora litoribus contraria, fluctibus undas
imprecor, arma armis; pugnent ipsique nepotesque.

The questions were asked: "Why might you have expected *fluctibus fluctus* in verse 628? Why was this impossible?" The first of these questions was quite generally answered correctly. The candidates noted the bearing of the words *litora litoribus* and *arma armis*. To the second question, however, there was given in a disconcertingly large number of cases an answer to which, as it was technically correct, we were obliged reluctantly to give credit: "Because it would spoil the meter." We could not prove that the writer of this answer was ignorant of the facts stated by not a few candidates, for example, "in such an arrangement as *fluctibus fluctus* the syllable *bus* would be lengthened by the consonants *fl* following, thus giving a cretic, a combination impossible in dactylic verse." Yet we entertained the gravest doubts of the actual possession of this knowledge by one who wrote only, "Because it would spoil the meter." Is it unreasonable to ask in behalf of the readers and in the interest of an intelligent control of facts that our pupils shall be educated to feel that on a written test in which no cross-examination is possible no answer can be regarded as adequate that demands another question for its comprehension? It is obvious that the readers cannot credit a candidate with knowledge of the meter and of specific ways in which it may be spoiled unless *details* are given.

As the result of my many years' experience of teaching and of observing in successive Junes the vagaries of the answer books presented at the examinations of the Board, I have become profoundly distrustful of all methods which lend themselves readily to mechanical use. I cannot bring myself to believe that these young minds are really deficient in intelligence. Nor can I believe that the teachers, on the whole, are not earnest and devoted. Yet despite the relatively good showing which Latin always makes among the examination subjects of the Board, the results are discouraging. Must we not bluntly ask ourselves the question, "Granted that our methods were adequate fifty years ago, are they adequate today, in an age in which the *distractions* that beset the path of our pupils cannot easily be properly described?" I commend to your reflections the admirable address of Principal George H. Browne, entitled "The Modern School and

Present-Day Distractions." [4] As he very truly says, "Only live fish can swim up stream in the present-day educational current." The stream is not of our choosing, but we must swim in it if we are to swim at all, and the conditions of success are fixed not by our own wishes but by the laws which govern the movement of its waters.

[4] *Education,* May, 1918.

THE QUEST OF INTELLIGENCE[1]

IN THE ESSAY on Lucretius with which Professor George Santayana opens his brilliant book, *Three Philosophical Poets,* he has occasion to define intelligence. It is, he says, " quickness in seeing things as they are." Now, the value of intelligence is indisputable. Who, whether young or old, whether teacher or pupil, does not instinctively like to regard himself as intelligent? Who, if he has a genuine interest in education, does not agree with Montesquieu in thinking that " the first motive which ought to impel us to study is the desire to augment the excellence of our nature and to render an intelligent being yet more intelligent "? It would seem to be almost a truism to say that the multiplication of intelligent men and women is indispensable in business, in the professions, in government, in a word, in all human intercourse. Yet an honest attempt to achieve intelligence, as Professor Santayana defines it, bristles with difficulties. Whether we read sober history or imaginative fiction, whether we scrutinize the behavior of our fellow beings or analyze our own mental and emotional processes, we shall find overwhelming evidence that only a small minority of mankind can normally " see things as they are." The great majority, as Caesar acutely observes in his *Commentaries on the Gallic War,* " are predisposed to believe in the truth of that which they ardently desire to be true," and instinctively clothe and disguise the real objective facts in the colors of their own personal likes and dislikes.

[1] Reprinted from *The Columbia Spectator,* Nov. 17, 1932.

Must we not say that such feeling, thinking, and action are marked by lack of intelligence?

Nevertheless, our disapprobation ought to be tempered by full recognition of the fact that it is very hard to be really intelligent. Consider a few simple and obvious facts. Each individual mind is the product of specific factors, due in part to heredity, in part to environment. The combinations of these factors are almost infinitely various, with resultant divergences of habits, tastes, ideals, everything, in fact, that is involved in self-expression. Such divergences are often strikingly noticeable in children whose parents are the same and who are reared together under the same general surroundings. These children — and " men are but children of a larger growth " — see things differently, feel differently, judge differently. Obviously, the things themselves as they really are remain the same; the things themselves cannot change to conform to these differences of opinion about their nature. Well did Aristotle say: " Those who would rightly judge the truth must be arbitrators not litigants." Science, which is the concrete proof of the existence of intelligence, is not merely a slowly increasing body of knowledge. It is the fruit of something even more important, a habit of the mind. As our own beloved Professor Woodbridge has finely said: " It is the habit of recognizing that there is a reasonable way of doing things as over against a passionate, impulsive, instinctive, or partisan way of doing things, and that this way is discoverable through inquiry." If anyone thinks that this is easy, let him make an honest test. He will find that it involves the most rigorous self-discipline. I doubt, in fact, whether anything short of a genuine passion for high excellence will enable him to continue the fight day after day against the influence of his personal instincts and his personal preferences.

Query: How highly do college students esteem intelligence? Upon the answer to this question depend in large measure our hopes for the future of America. For it is you who should provide the sorely needed insight into things as they really are. The author of *Proverbs* in the Old Testament is surely justified in saying: " Where there is no vision, the people perish."

ACADEMIC LETTERS
1911–1936

I

Periucundae nobis fuerunt litterae vestrae quibus tot tantasque res per annos iam centum felicissime gestas celebraturi nos ad ferias saeculares vocare tam benigne voluistis. Gaudemus quod et vos et ii quos prioribus annis in Academia vestra adlexit rerum cognitio ita operam navastis ut laus atque gloria bonarum artium magis magisque eluxerit, neque dubitamus quin, ut olim, sic in reliquum tempus vos cum de vita hominum tum de scientia ipsa optime meritos studia gratorum civium semper prosecutura sint. Nam quis oblivisci potest quantum in philosophia illuminanda profecerit Monrad ille, in historia conscribenda Munch, in doctrina zoologica explicanda Sars? Quid quod in rebus magneticis Hansteen, in mathematicis Abel inter omnes eminuit? Neque alii ingeniis uberrimis Academiam vestram non exornaverunt. Optimo vobis iure in saeculo iam exacto gloriari licet, optimo iure spem summam concipere in saeculum venturum.

Vestrae igitur voluntati obsecuti, unum e professoribus nostris, Guilelmum Henricum Carpenter, virum et ipsum eruditissimum necnon in rebus academicis penitus versatum legatum constituimus qui hanc gratulationem nostram vobis rite significaret. Valete.

Dabamus Novi Eboraci a. d. vii Idus Iunias Anno Salutis MCMXI.

II

CVRATORES
VNIVERSITATIS · COLVMBIAE
IN · VRBE · NOVO · EBORACO · SITAE
RECTORI · MAGNIFICO · SENATVIQVE · ACADEMICO
VNIVERSITATIS · REGIAE
VRATISLAVIENSIS
S · P · D

Litteris vestris, viri doctissimi, ad nos nuper perlatis libenter cognovimus vos annum centesimum ab eo quo ex Academiis duabus iam tum in omni genere doctrinae multum et diu versatis Vniversitas vestra auspiciis optimis constituta exstitisset feriis saecularibus esse celebraturos. Nihil ergo antiquius habuimus quam ut vobis et gratularemur et gratias ex animo ageremus quod nos quoque illo optimo dierum hospitio accipere voluissetis. Iuvat Academiam vestram, vasto quidem gurgite Oceani a nobis disiunctam sed tamen ea quasi cognatione qua inter se continentur omnes veri indagatores nobiscum maxime coniunctam, in orbis terrae memoriam sempiternam adeo multa iam disseminasse. Nam cuiuscumque sive artis sive scientiae annales inspicere libet, non fieri potest quin inveniantur eorum nomina qui apud vos plurimum in communem fructum contulerunt, Bunsen, Kirchhoff, Cohn, Göppert, Westphal, von der Hagen, Rückert, Kölbing, Stenzel, Neumann, Purkinje, Cohnheim, Stobbe — sed vix possumus omnes percensere. Peractis utinam vel maiora instent!

Hoc gaudium auguriumque nostrum ut ad vos rite perferretur, unum e professoribus nostris, Guilelmum

Henricum Carpenter, virum et ipsum studiis philologis eruditissimum necnon ad hoc munus maxime idoneum, legatum delegimus. Valete.

Dabamus Novi Eboraci a. d. vii Idus Iunias Anno Salutis MCMXI.

III

VNIVERSITAS · COLVMBIAE
IN · VRBE · NOVO · EBORACO · SITA
VNIVERSITATI · SANCTI · ANDREAE
DIEM · NATALEM · QVINGENTESIMVM · FERIIS
CELEBRATVRAE
S · P · D

Laeto gratoque animo, viri clarissimi, litteras vestras nuper accepimus quibus nos vocavistis ut caerimoniis vestris quingenariis interessemus.

Qua de re nobis saepe cogitantibus et memoria tenentibus ad quantam studiorum gloriam Vniversitas vestra esset per saeculorum seriem evecta, quot ibi de scientia optime meriti essent professores, quot inde prodissent alumni qui alius aliter rei publicae inservirent, evenit ut vim ipsam educationis non satis admirari possemus. Omnino fuerunt qui disciplinae expertes innata ingeni praestantia plurimum valuerint. Sed tamen optimo iure contendit Cicero cum ad naturam eximiam atque illustrem accesserit ratio quaedam conformatioque doctrinae, tum illud nescio quid praeclarum ac singulare solere existere. Ex hoc intellegi potest quanto quamque liberali munere fungantur qui adulescentes doceant. Quod quidem munus vos sane insigniter sustinuistis. Idcirco enim litterarum sedem exornavistis ut inde profecti discipuli vestri vitam hominum rudem olim et necessariis modo artificiis excultam ad elegantiora deducerent.

Haec omnia cum animo reputaremus, Nicholaum Murray Butler, huius Vniversitatis Praesidem, ad vos legavimus, quo viro neminem in omni ratione atque usu instituendi exercitatiorem habemus, neminem e nostro doctorum coetu magis dilectum. Hic et vobiscum simul quinque illa saecula esse felicissime peracta gaudebit et omnium nostrum nomine initia sexti gratulabitur auspicatissima.

Per annos utinam labentes res vobis ita succedat ut operae istius ac fidei in artibus ingenuis illustrandis iam adeo praeclare adhibitae cum vestrates tum quicumque in aliis terris litterarum humaniorum amore tenentur fructus percipiant uberrimos. Valete.

Dabamus Novi Eboraci Idibus Iuliis Anno Salutis MDCCCCXI.

IV

Perquam nobis acceptum exoptatumque accidit quod nos eorum sollemnium testes participesque esse voluistis quibus diem natalem Societatis vestrae per annos iam ducentos quinquaginta in scientia naturali promovenda florentis propediem celebraturi essetis. Neque enim fieri poterat quin series illa mirabilis rerum inventarum per quas toti generi humano non solum via et ratio naturam complectendi sed etiam vitae condicio cottidianae tantum in melius mutata esset, nos quoque penitus commoveret. Nam si primam memoriam ordinis vestri repetere libet et recordari quam longe aliter de specie et ratione naturae illo atque hoc tempore homines vulgo senserint, difficile est iis satis digne gratias agere qui ingeniis studiisque effecerunt ut hodie et qualia sint foedera naturae tanto subtilius intellegamus et qualis necessitudo inter hominem ipsum et universam naturam intercedat tanto liberius iudicemus.

Longum est neque vero hoc loco necesse — eminent enim omnibusque qui sapiunt in ore sunt — eos recensere paene innumerabiles qui vestrae Societatis sodales se in caecas veri latebras insinuaverunt atque inde victores quid fieri posset, quid nequiret rettulerunt. Duo autem, Carolus Lyell et Carolus Darwin, summo ingenio praestantes, nullius, ut vobis moris est, addicti iurare in verba magistri, rerum cognoscere causas tam feliciter potuerunt ut si quis reperta eorum praetermittere velit, nullo iam modo neque de hoc orbe terrae neque de vi et natura animantium neque de ipsa omnium hominum consortione quicquam recte cogitare queat. Hi et tot alii ex ordine vestro illustrissimo vitam humanam per inventas artes excoluerunt omnesque sui memores iure fecerunt merendo. Namque eos, ut ait Lucretius divinus ille poeta,

usus et impigrae simul experientia mentis
paulatim docuit pedetemptim progredientes.
Sic unum quicquid paulatim protrahit aetas
in medium ratioque in luminis erigit oras.

Itaque libenter vobis morigerantes, Nicholaum Murray Butler, Universitatis nostrae praesidem, virum et multiplici ingenio praeditum et, ut verbis Evelyn vestri utamur, omnia explorare meliora retinere solitum, ad vos legavimus per quem velut praesentes et vobis partam gloriam gratularemur et ut peractis paria essent futura saecula exoptaremus. Valete.

Dabamus Novi Eboraci Idibus Iuniis Anno Salutis MDCCCCXII.

V

CVRATORES
VNIVERSITATIS · COLVMBIAE
IN · VRBE · NOVO · EBORACO · SITAE
RECTORI · ET · SENATVI
VNIVERSITATIS · GRONINGANAE
S · P · D

Litteras vestras, viri insignes, libenter accepimus quibus memoriam Academiae vestrae abhinc annos trecentos apertae recognituri nos tam comiter invitastis ut ad ferias illas saeculares sodalem e nostro doctorum coetu mitteremus. Neque vero fieri potuit quin gauderemus vos tam diu in bonis artibus et docendis et promovendis tanta cum laude esse versatos. Nam non solum ea rerum societate vobiscum coniuncti sumus qua omnes studiis liberalibus dediti inter se continentur. Est etiam vetus alia necessitudo quae inter Bataviam et nostram aulam intercedit. Urbs enim ipsa in qua sita est Universitas nostra priore nomine semper nos de iis fortibus strenuisque Batavis commonefacit qui nomen Amstelodami iterum in nova terra illustrare studuerunt. Nec sine causa rem sic gesserunt. Iam tum libertati, qua remota nulla civitas ad summam gloriam scientiae iustitiaeque potuit efflorescere, sedes amplissima erat apud vestrates parata, ratioque quasi quaedam lux vitae humanae tenebras discutere iterum adsuescebat. Quibus in tenebris dum maiores vestri viam stabilem dispicere conabantur, verbum Domini, ut erat in antiquo sigillo vestro inscriptum, pedibus lucerna fuit. Nos autem, a vobis vasto maris spatio longe disiuncti, eodem tamen animo iam diu laboramus, si forte in Eius lumine videamus lumen. Et quidem optimo iure omnes in magnam spem venimus hanc mentis caliginem totam fore dispulsam. Nam ex quo cum in aliis partibus Europae tum praecipue apud Batavos litterae humaniores tamquam renasci coeperunt, ita claruit, ut sententia quadam nobili Lucretiana utamur, aliud ex alio ut iam ultima naturae nos aliquando pervidere posse confidamus.

His omnibus rationibus adducti Guilelmum Henricum Carpenter, huic Universitati praepositum, virum in consilio dando prudentissimum, in negotiis academicis obeundis indefessum, ad vos legavimus qui nostrum omnium nomine vobis gratularetur et hospes vester ludis illis triduanis laetus interesset. Valete.

Dabamus Novi Eboraci a. d. iii Nonas Iunias Anno Salutis MCMXIV.

VI

PRAESES · CVRATORES · PROFESSORES
VNIVERSITATIS · COLVMBIAE
IN · VRBE · NOVO · EBORACO · SITAE
RECTORI · MAGNIFICO · SENATVIQVE · ACADEMICO
VNIVERSITATIS · REGALIS · NEAPOLITANAE
S · P · D

Rem nobis periucundam fecistis, viri clarissimi, cum
memoriam Academiae vestrae abhinc annos iam septin-
gentos conditae recognituri nos laetitiae istius et testes
et participes esse tam comiter voluistis. Neque vero fieri
potuit quin gauderemus vos per tot saecula in bonis artibus et docendis et promovendis tanta cum laude esse versatos. Nihil enim est quo artius homines inter se concili-
entur quam vero scientiarum amore. Tum demum silent
gentium diversitates, silent etiam factionum clamores,
eloquitur tantum una eademque veritas.

Olim in vestra Aula praeclare, ne dicam angelice,
profitebatur philosophiam illam Aristoteliam Sanctus
Thomas Aquinas; apud recentiores summo et ingenio et
in patriam pietate elucebant De Sanctis, Pessina, Set-
tembrini. Quam multi labentibus annis intercedebant
qui de scientia optime meriti sunt! Quam multi hodie
studiis vestris insigniter inserviunt!

Haec omnia cum animo reputaremus, tres viros ido-
neos e nostro doctorum coetu ad vos legavimus per quos
nostrum omnium nomine et Italiam laudibus cum artium tum virorum nobilium cumulatam et Neapolim,
secessum Vergilio poetarum principi dilectissimum se-

demque Musarum omnium amoenissimam excultissi-
mamque velut ipsi praesentes salutaremus et ut peractis
paria essent futura saecula exoptaremus. Valete.

Dabamus Novi Eboraci Nonis Aprilibus Anno Salutis
MCMXXIV.

VII

VNIVERSITATI · HEBRAEAE
HIEROSOLYMITANAE
S · P · D
VNIVERSITAS · COLVMBIAE
IN · VRBE · NOVO · EBORACO · SITA

Litteras vestras, viri nobiscum scientiarum omnium studiis consociati, modo perlegimus in quibus feriis illis quas Kalendis Aprilibus proximis acturi estis nos quoque interesse tam benigne voluistis. Gratulamur vobis quod novam Academiam vestram, feliciter conditam, laetis iam animis aspicitis. Iuvat quod tandem eos hospitio accipere parati estis qui cognitionis amore instincti ita institui cupiunt ut vitam humanam per inventas artes excolere possint omnesque sui memores facere merendo. Iuvat quod vos, eius gentis progenies, qua ex gente tam clara lux religionis humano generi semper se diffudit, posthac in urbe Hierosolymis doctrinae multiplicis lumen splendidum omnibus praeferetis.

Hac de re nobis reputantibus in memoriam redierunt versus illi Horatiani:

> Fortes creantur fortibus et bonis;
> doctrina sed vim promovet insitam.

Itaque auguramur, nec nos fallit augurium, de iis qui quacumque in parte orbis terrarum versantur operam impense dant ut salus atque concordia omnium hominum magis magisque confirmentur, vos optime esse merituros. Quem quidem fructum laborum utinam Academia vestra labentibus annis uberiorem atque laetiorem percipiat! Valete.

Dabamus Novi Eboraci Idibus Martiis Anno Salutis MCMXXV.

VIII

VNIVERSITAS · COLVMBIAE
IN · VRBE · NOVO · EBORACO · SITA
VNIVERSITATI · STVDIORVM · TICINENSI
VNDECIMAS · FERIAS · SAECVLARES · SVAE
INSTITVTIONIS · SOLLEMNITER · ACTVRAE
S · P · D

Perquam nobis, viri clarissimi, acceptum accidit quod nos earum feriarum testes participesque esse voluistis quibus memoriam Academiae vestrae per annos iam mille et centum in omnibus ingenuis artibus cum docendis tum in maius promovendis felicissime versatae propediem recognituri essetis. Nihil ergo antiquius habuimus quam ut vobis ex animo et gratias ageremus et gratularemur per tot saeculorum seriem in ista sede amplissima doctrinarum apud vestrates constituta numquam defuisse qui ingeniis instincti studiisque vitam hominum rudem olim et necessariis modo artificiis excultam ad elegantiora deducere conarentur. Namque eos, ut ait Lucretius divinus ille poeta,

> usus et impigrae simul experientia mentis
> paulatim docuit pedetemptim progredientes.
> Sic unum quicquid paulatim protrahit aetas
> in medium ratioque in luminis erigit oras.

Huic luciferae rationi, ut maiores vestri, sic nostri semper penitus dediti fuerunt. Est enim ea quasi quaedam lux, a Deo ipso profecta, quae ad tenebras vitae humanae in primis valeat discutiendas. Unde efficitur ut eodem quo priores illi animo nos recentiores verum etiam nunc in-

dagemur si forte, ut est in antiquo sigillo nostro inscriptum, in Eius lumine videamus lumen.

Vestrae igitur voluntati libenter obsecuti, unum e nostro doctorum coetu, Dino Bigongiari, virum et ipsum
Italo genere ortum et in historia litterisque Italiae eruditissimum adlegavimus, qui et vobiscum simul undecim
illa saecula esse tam luculenter peracta gauderet et nostrum omnium nomine initia duodecimi salutaret auspicatissima. Valete.

Dabamus Novi Eboraci a. d. x Kalendas Maias Anno
Salutis MCMXXV.

IX

VNIVERSITAS · COLVMBIAE
NOVEBORACENSIS
VNIVERSITATIS · COLLEGIO
LONDINIENSI
S · P · D

Periucundae nobis fuerunt litterae vestrae quibus tot tantasque res per annos iam centum felicissime gestas celebraturi nos laetitiae istius et testes et participes esse tam comiter voluistis. Quibus feriis ut tamquam praesentes frueremur omnes, quam libenter, quippe qui vobiscum stirpe, lingua, studiis coniuncti essemus, voluntati vestrae non deesse decrevimus!

Iuvat enim pie colere meritisque laudibus efferre

cognatas urbes populosque propinquos.

Iuvat recognoscere eos studiosos paene innumerabiles qui sive in Britannia sive in America ex sedibus Musarum ad munera vitae suscipienda prodierunt, si forte ingenuas illas promoverent artes quae ad salutem et concordiam totius generis humani pertinerent. Nam ex illis demum studiis effloruit ea libertas cum mentis tum rei publicae qua communiter vobiscum iam diu utimur. Hanc libertatem nobis saepe numero cogitantibus in memoriam redit praeclarum illud quod apud Marcum Aurelium Antoninum legere possis:

φαντασίαν λαβεῖν πολιτείας ἰσονόμου κατ᾽ ἰσότητα καὶ ἰσηγορίαν διοικουμένης, καὶ βασιλείας τιμώσης πάντων μάλιστα τὴν ἐλευθερίαν τῶν ἀρχομένων.

Hanc libertatem utinam scientia rerum quae sola aperuit qualis intercedat necessitudo inter hominem ipsum et universam naturam magis magisque confirmet atque tueatur!

Vestrae igitur voluntati obsecuti, unum e professoribus nostris, Georgium Philippum Krapp, virum et ipsum in lingua litterisque Anglicis eruditissimum et ad hoc munus praecipue idoneum, legatum nunc constituimus per quem et vobis iam partam dignitatem gratularemur et ut peracto vel uberiora essent saecula futura exoptaremus. Valete.

Dabamus Novi Eboraci Kalendis Iuniis Anno Salutis MCMXXVII.

X

VNIVERSITAS · COLVMBIAE
NOVEBORACENSIS
VNIVERSITATI · TORONTONENSI
S · P · D

Litteras vestras, viri doctissimi, nuper laeti accepimus
in quibus memoriam Academiae vestrae abhinc annos
centum conditae mox recognituri nos quoque feriis illis
interesse comiter voluistis. Neque vero fieri potuit quin
gauderemus vos, nobiscum et scientiarum studiis et omnibus moribus pacis amicitiaeque consociatos, tam diu
in ingenuis artibus modo sollerter docendis modo in
maius promovendis tanta cum laude esse versatos. Est
enim vetus quaedam necessitudo quae inter vestrates et
nostram aulam intercedit. Utrique regiae eidem domui
privilegia nostra debemus; utrisque cordi est nomen
antiquum Collegii Regalis. Accedebat quod ea tempora
reputantes nos penitus commovit series illa mirabilis
rerum inventarum per quas labentibus annis toti generi
humano non solum via et ratio naturam complectendi
sed etiam vitae condicio cottidianae tantum mutatae
sunt. Haec veri indagatio prout usquequaque vigebit,
talia pro se quaeque gens ad communem fructum poterit
conferre ut in omni rerum humanarum mutatione quae-
cumque annis labentibus oblata erit mutuis tamen inter
se beneficiis devincti teneri possint omnes.

Vestrae igitur voluntati obsecuti unum e decanis nostris Fridericum I. E. Woodbridge, virum et collegis et
discipulis dilectissimum, qui, cum credat, ut ait Plato

ille, ὅπῃ ἂν ὁ λόγος ὥσπερ πνεῦμα φέρῃ, ταύτῃ ἰτέον, et aliis viam monstrat et ipse semper praecedit, legatum constituimus per quem vobis velut praesentes et saeculum illud esse tam luculenter peractum gratularemur et in posterum quoque omnia fausta feliciaque exoptaremus. Valete.

Dabamus Novi Eboraci Kalendis Octobribus Anno Salutis MCMXXVII.

XI

VNIVERSITAS · COLVMBIAE
IN · VRBE · NOVO · EBORACO · SITA
VNIVERSITATI · PORTORICENSI
S · P · D

Rem nobis pergratam fecistis, viri doctissimi, quod res gestas Universitatis vestrae abhinc annos quinque et viginti conditae celebraturi nos quoque feriis illis interesse tam benigne voluistis. Rediit enim in memoriam nobis vox praeclara Aristotelis: πάντες ἄνθρωποι τοῦ εἰδέναι ὀέργονται φύσει. Hic cognoscendi appetitus quo acrius apud vestros cives vigeret atque expleretur, in artes per hos annos in primis necessarias explicandas maximo cum fructu ita incubuistis ut litterae humaniores non iacerent neglectae.

Gaudemus nobis licere una vobiscum laborare ut iis morbis pestibusque quae maxime in terris soli propinquis vitam hominum in discrimen adducant ex insula vestra exturbatis sana corpora ad mentes sanas valeant efficiendas. Gaudemus nos amicos amicorum operae participes in vestra aula linguam litterasque Hispanas docere atque excolere posse. Quin etiam magnam spem concepimus fore ut vos, quippe qui et originem ab antiquissimo cultu Europae repetatis et iam nostrae recentioris rei publicae Americanae in partem deveneritis, in ista amoenitate terrae marisque sedem studiorum utriusque cultus propriam instituere possitis quo undique et discendi et investigandi causa conveniant iuvenes ingeniosi. De quo consilio, ut verbis utamur Tibulli, poetae elegantissimi,

Hoc precor, hunc illum nobis Aurora nitentem
Luciferum roseis candida portet equis.

Haec omnia cum animo reputaremus, unum e decanis nostris Fridericum I. E. Woodbridge, virum in studiis academicis impigerrimum, ad vos legavimus. Hic, quem voce quadam Heracliti summo iure describere videamur posse, Εἷς ἐμοὶ μύριοι ἐὰν ἄριστος ᾗ, et vobis iam famam contigisse tantam gratulabitur et in posterum omnia bona faustaque ex animo exoptabit. Valete.

Dabamus Novi Eboraci Kalendis Martiis Anno Salutis MCMXXVIII.

XII

SOCIETAS · CLASSICA
NOVEBORACENSIS
ANDREAE · FLEMING · WEST
S · P · D

Cum tu, vir utriusque linguae litterate peritus, tot annis feliciter exactis, otium cum dignitate coniunctum tandem ineas, nos quibus cordi sunt eadem studia, aliquam tibi nostri amoris significationem facere voluimus. Iuvat recensere quantum ita profeceris ut laus et gloria bonarum artium eluceret. Iuvat tuae vitae fastos diligenter evolvere per quam omnes tui memores fecisti merendo. Itaque tibi gratulantes exoptamus ut vesperascente vitae luce amore eorum qui a te instincti patriae civibusque prodesse cupiunt diu perfruare. Vale.

Dabamus Novi Eboraci a. d. xv Kal. Dec. Anno Salutis MCMXXVIII.

XIII

VNIVERSITAS · COLVMBIAE
IN · VRBE · NOVO · EBORACO · SITA
COLLEGIO · RADCLIFFIANO
S · P · D

Litteras vestras, collegae insignes, libenter nuper perlegimus quibus sacra vestra semisaecularia mox celebraturi nos quoque feriis illis interesse tam benigne voluistis.
Nihil ergo antiquius habuimus quam ut vobis ex animo
et gratias ageremus et gratularemur per hos quinquaginta annos ex aula vestra prodisse tot feminas quae
scienter institutae vitam hominum ingenuis artibus ex-
colerent. Omnino fuerunt quae disciplinae expertes innata indolis praestantia multum ad communem fructum
adtulerint. Sed tamen optimo iure contendit Tullius cum
ad naturam eximiam accesserit conformatio doctrinae,
tum praeclarum quiddam existere posse. Ex illa demum
doctrina effloruit haec et mentis et rei publicae libertas
qua communiter vobiscum iam diu utimur. Peractis utinam vel maiora instent!

Vestrae igitur voluntati obsecuti, Collegi Barnardini
decanam, Virginiam Crocheron Gildersleeve, feminam et
ipsam eruditissimam et in ratione usuque instituendi
penitus versatam, ad vos legavimus quae nostrum omnium nomine vobis gratularetur et in posterum omnia
fausta feliciaque exoptaret. Valete.

Dabamus Novi Eboraci Idibus Maiis Anno Salutis
MCMXXIX.

XIV

VNIVERSITAS · COLVMBIAE
IN · VRBE · NOVO · EBORACO · SITA
VNIVERSITATI · RVTGERSENSI
S · P · D

Litteras vestras, viri doctissimi, libenter accepimus quibus eventus vestratium rei rusticae studiorum per annos iam quinquaginta feliciter cultorum recognituri nostram quoque Academiam feriis illis interesse voluistis. Nihil ergo antiquius habuimus quam ut vobis significaremus quanti istos tam sollertes atque fructuosos labores faceremus. Nam, ut ait Tullius, agro bene culto nihil potest esse nec usu uberius nec specie ornatius. Itaque vos qui experimentis scienter instituendis terrae vim ac naturam subtilius intellegere iam diu studetis ut eius munera divina ad modum et certiorem et ampliorem reddantur, beneficium adfertis quod ad victum et salutem omnium qui ubique sunt maxime pertinet.

Vestrae igitur voluntati obsecuti, unum e professoribus nostris O. S. Morgan, Ph.D., virum et ipsum in ratione usuque agri culturae eruditissimum et ad hoc munus praecipue idoneum, legatum nunc constituimus per quem et vobis iam partam dignitatem gratularemur et ut peractis vel uberiores essent anni futuri exoptaremus. Valete.

Dabamus Novi Eboraci Nonis Octobribus Anno Domini MCMXXX.

XV

VNIVERSITAS · COLVMBIAE
IN · VRBE · NOVO · EBORACO · SITA
VNIVERSITATI · GEORGIAE · WASHINGTONIANAE
S · P · D

Rem nobis gratam fecistis, viri doctissimi, cum diem natalem ducentesimum illius civis perillustris cuius in honorem vestra ipsorum Aula nominata est, eximiis caerimoniis mox celebraturi nos quoque sacris istis interesse tam comiter voluistis. Cuius quidem viri quam memoriter omnes Americani, ne dicamus omnes libertatis amantes qui ubique sunt, gravitatem, fidem, praestantem in re publica conservanda prudentiam praedicant! Nobis enim in memoriam redit Ennianum illud:

> Noenum rumores ponebat ante salutem.
> Ergo postque magisque viri nunc gloria claret.

Iustus ac tenax propositi, et non modo rei militaris sed etiam rationum pacis peritissimus quantum ille patriae profuerit semper in ore omnibus erit. Gaudemus igitur nobis iam licere simul vobiscum illum Washington omni laude cumulare

> quo nihil maius meliusve terris
> fata donavere bonique divi
> nec dabunt, quamvis redeant in aurum
> tempora priscum.

Itaque vestrae voluntati obsecuti, unum e nostro doctorum coetu, Marcus Benjamin, Sc.D., LL.D., virum et ipsum cognitione rerum insignem et ad hoc munus praecipue idoneum, ad vos legavimus per quem nos omnes laetitiae vestrae participes esse possemus. Valete.

Dabamus Novi Eboraci Idibus Februariis Anno Salutis MCMXXXII.

XVI

VNIVERSITAS · COLVMBIAE
IN · VRBE · NOVO · EBORACO · SITA
SOCIETATI · GOETHIANAE
S · P · D

Rem nobis pergratam fecistis, viri doctissimi, quod memoriam illius Goethe, quo nemo poeta apud Germanos exstitit magis perfectus atque absolutus, prope diem recognituri nos quoque sacris vestris interesse tam comiter voluistis. Quamquam enim anni sunt iam centum ex quo ille de vita decessit, tamen adhuc vivit vigetque per ora omnium quibus sunt cordi et litterae et magnitudo mentis; neque vero dubium est quin illius famam imminuere possit nec innumerabilis annorum series nec fuga temporum. Cuius quidem viri ingenium proprium, acutum, praeter modum multiplex cum reputamus, non satis admirari possumus vel vim animi innatam vel eam rerum cognitionem qua sese facile principem praestitit. In studia quam diversa impigre incubuit! Quam subtiliter metamorphoses plantarum inspiciebat! Quanto animi ardore suam ipsius colorum doctrinam defendebat! Quam intellegenter sonorum suavium concentu fruebatur! In poesi et lyrica et scaenica difficile est dictu quanta dulcedine, quanta sublimitate sibi omnium animos soleat conciliare. Quemnam *Faustus* non ita commovet ut elatius intellegat qualis necessitudo inter hominem ipsum et universam naturam intercedat? Quid de iis fabulis dicamus quibus poetarum ritu commentus mores adfectionesque hominum oratione soluta depinxit? Optimo iure

Goethe in numerum eorum ascitus est qui vitam humanam mirum in modum excoluerunt omnesque sui memores fecerunt merendo.

Itaque libenter vobis morigerantes Fridericum I. E. Woodbridge, LL.D., virum et ipsum artium liberalium peritissimum et vobis praecipue acceptum, legatum constituimus qui nomine nostrum omnium memoriam tanti ingeni hac quasi laureola honoraret.

Dabamus Novi Eboraci Kalendis Martiis Anno Salutis MCMXXXII.

XVII

VNIVERSITAS · COLVMBIAE
IN · VRBE · NOVO · EBORACO · SITA
SOCIETATI · SPINOZANAE
S · P · D

Litteras vestras, viri doctissimi, libenter accepimus quibus memoriam Benedicti de Spinoza, quo nemo certe in doctrina exhibenda philosophica simplicior exstitit sinceriorque, nemo veri cernendi appetentior, mox recognituri nos quoque sacris vestris interesse tam benigne voluistis. Haud vero immemores sumus quantam labentibus annis gloriam ille adeptus sit qui ipse secretum iter insistere mallet et semitam vitae fallentis. Cum autem sic vitam teneret umbratilem, tamen et praesensit quae duce rerum naturae cognitione rationibus hominum iam tum ingrueret mutatio et non modo intellegentiam ad res humanas ac divinas complectendas adhibere potuit sed etiam ad eas novo quodam pacto ordinandas tuendasque fortitudinem.

Quanta quidem animi elatione adficimur cum eum librum legimus qui *Tractatus Theologico-Politicus* inscribitur, perspicimusque quid inter religionem et philosophiam intersit! Quid de *Ethica* dicamus, quo opere praeclaro ille vir ardenti Dei amore instinctus dilucide ordine geometrico patefecit et qualis necessitudo inter Deum ipsum et universam naturam intercedat et quem ad modum ex amore Dei intellectuali nascatur nobis beatitudo? Quam multos, et philosophos et poetas et re-

ligiosos, per hosce annos docuit, delectavit, commovit
eius tam subtilis, tam excelsa ars disserendi!

Vestrae igitur voluntati obsecuti unum e nostro doctorum coetu Irwin Edman, Ph.D., virum et ipsum disciplinae philosophicae litterate peritissimum et ex eius
propriis studiis ad hoc munus praecipue idoneum, ad vos
legavimus per quem memoriam illius praepotentis ingeni
pie honoraremus.

Dabamus Novi Eboraci Nonis Augustis Anno Salutis MCMXXXII.

XVIII

PRAESES · CVRATORES · ORDINES
VNIVERSITATIS · COLVMBIAE
IN · VRBE · NOVO · EBORACO · SITAE
AB · INITIO · NOMINE · COLLEGII · REGALIS · NVNCVPATAE
QVIPPE · QVAE · ANNO · MILLESIMO · SEPTINGENTESIMO
QVINQVAGESIMO · QVARTO · DIPLOMATE · REGIO · GEORGII
SECVNDI · ANGLIAE · REGIS · IN · PROVINCIA
NOVEBORACENSI · ESSET · CONSTITVTA

SOCIIS · ACADEMIAE · GALLICAE
A · VIRO · ET · LITTERARVM · ET · RERVM · GESTARVM · LAVDE
PERILLVSTRI · CARDINALI · DVCE · DE · RICHELIEV · EX · VM-
BRACVLIS · IN · LVMINIS · ORAS · EVOCATAE · QVAE · VIAM
AD · IMMORTALITATEM · FERENTEM · INGREDERETVR
FERIAS · IAM · TRECENTESIMAS · INSTITVTIONIS
SVAE · SOLLEMNITER · ACTVRAE
SALVTEM · PLVRIMAM · DICVNT

Vos, viri praeclarissimi, quibus est cordi oratio pura
ac dilucida eademque multiplex, quibus per saecula iam
tria propositum est inconcinnitatem sermonis cottidiani
genere dicendi commutare exquisitiore eoque modo elegantias vitae exaugere, quam libenter, quam laetis animis salutamus! Nobis enim in memoriam redit vox illa
quam e dictis Democriti protulit Plutarchus: λόγος γὰρ
ἔργου σκιή. Hoc Democritium si attentius reputaveris,
negari non poterit quin in umbris insit certa fallendi po-
testas. Si quis igitur sive in cognitione naturae dissemi-
nanda sive in litteris excolendis rei publicae pro virili
parte voluerit prodesse, effingat oportebit dictionem per-
spicuam, subtilem, ipsam rerum veritatem exprimentem.

Ille, ut ait Horatius, cui perite suadenti hoc potissimum anno auscultare debemus,

> cum tabulis animum censoris sumet honesti;
> audebit, quaecumque parum splendoris habebunt
> et sine pondere erunt et honore indigna ferentur,
> verba movere loco. . . .
> Vemens et liquidus puroque simillimus amni
> fundet opes patriamque beabit divite lingua.

Neque vero deerit Lexicon sollerter confectum unde tamquam ex thesauro rerum pretiosarum locutiones idoneas depromere possis quibus mores sententiaeque populi perpoliti proprie luculenterque exprimi queant.

Hoc tam amplo tamque utili munere sermonem ad normam dirigendi Academia vestra labentibus annis sic est perfuncta ut vix satis digne eam possimus laudare. His feliciter peractis utinam vel maiora instent!

Sed nos eodem praestantiae studio quo vestrates commovemur. Unde consentaneum est societatem nostram et docentium et discentium instituta, linguam litterasque patriae vestrae plurimi fecisse. Namque cum in annales vestros animum intendimus, gentem agnoscimus fortem, ingeniosam, libertatis appetentem, quae necessariis artificiis non neglectis elegantias tamen vitae numquam non praeposuerit. Libenti igitur animo Praesidem huiusce Universitatis, Nicholaum Murray Butler, virum inter socios vestri ipsorum Instituti illustris ascitum, quippe qui ingenio, eruditione, sapientia usque quaque habeatur praestantissimus, legatum ad vos constituimus. Valete.

Dabamus Novi Eboraci Nonis Iuniis Anno Salutis MCMXXXV.

XIX

VNIVERSITAS · COLVMBIAE
IN · VRBE · NOVO · EBORACO · SITA
SOCIIS · EXPLORATIONIS · MVSEIQVE · GEOLOGICI
MAGNAE · BRITANNIAE
IAM · RES · PER · ANNOS · CENTVM · FELICITER · GESTAS
RECOGNITVRIS
SALVTEM · PLVRIMAM · DICIT

Epistulam eam libenter accepimus quam pro vobis, viri in officina daedalae Naturae perite versati, trans Oceanum, non iam ut olim dissociabilem, nuper ad nos tam comiter misit Dominus Praeses Honoratissimi Consilii Intimi Suae Maiestatis. Non enim fieri potuit quin gauderemus vestrates post annos centum exactos consilia equitis illius perillustris Henrici Thomae De la Beche, qui primus spem status geologici Insularum Britannicarum explorandi fortiter scienterque concepit, etiam nunc animis exsequi atque amplificare indefessis. Cuius ex memoria excidere possunt eorum nomina quos posteritas pro conditoribus vestrae famae optimo iure habebit? Piis animis et nunc coluntur et labentibus annis colentur (ut paucos e permultis commemoremus), De la Beche ipse, Forbes, Phillips, Ramsay, Selwyn, Aveline, Playfair, Gibbs, Jukes, Smyth, Murchison, Oldham, Bristow, Lowry, Geikie, Salter, Hull, omnes de patria optime meriti. Nos eadem laude qua vos illos insignes viros efferimus qui multiplici ingenio, multiplici cognitione rerum naturae instincti testimonia saxorum sagaciter exquisita in ordinem redegerunt subtiliterque interpretati sunt ut confectionem chartae geologicae atque agronomicae totius regni gradatim propius ad summam manum perducerent.

Illud quoque nobis admirationem movet quod ad has difficiles quaestiones geologicas explicandas tot diversas scientias adhibuistis. Vestris enim ipsorum studiis opem tulerunt ii qui singuli in scientia botanica, chemica, zoologica, palaeontologica exstiterunt eruditissimi. Quibus de causis vobis ex animo gratulamur quod ad vestras opes novum aedificium adiuncturi estis unde ex antiquis thesauris scientiae geologicae ea commoda vel uberius possitis proferre quae ad communem utilitatem vitae hodiernae conducant.

Haec omnia cum animo reputaremus, Praesidem huius Universitatis, Nicholaum Murray Butler, virum doctissimum a quo nihil neque rationis neque usus Anglici alienum est, legatum constituimus qui vobis et benevolentiam nostram significaret et omnia fausta in posterum exoptaret. Valete.

Dabamus Novi Eboraci Idibus Iuniis Anno Salutis MCMXXXV.

XX

PRAESES · CVRATORES · ORDINES
VNIVERSITATIS · COLVMBIAE
IN · VRBE · NOVO · EBORACO · SITAE
RECTORI · SENATVI · DOCTORIBVS
VNIVERSITATIS · ROMANI · STVDI
S · P · D

Vos, viri doctissimi, custodes atque auctores eius
domus artium scientiarumque ingenuarum existima-
tionis cui aptissime impositum est nomen Sapientiae,
quam libenter, quam piis animis salutamus! Nobis enim
ante oculos obversatur ea longa annorum series quibus,
cum rebus humanis magnas gravesque deinceps muta-
tiones adferrent, vestra tamen Universitas averti non
potuit quin suis propriis muneribus veri sagaciter in-
quirendi tranquilla mente fungeretur. Iuvat recordari
quanta in vestrum Studium beneficia olim contulerint illi
amore disciplinarum liberalium commoti Pontifices
Maximi, Bonifatius VIII, Eugenius IV, Alexander VI.
Iuvat nunc de novo spatiosoque domicilio, vestra rerum
gestarum amplitudine dignissimo, certiores fieri in quod,
quasi in fines late extentos, munificentia locupletati Suae
Maiestatis Victoris Emmanuelis III et Beniti Mussolini
rei publicae rectoris insignis, laetis animis ingressuri
estis. Felix utinam faustaque sit et vobis et almae Urbi
et omnibus qui ubique sunt dies illa dedicationis!

Vestrae igitur voluntati, nuper nobis tam comiter ex-
positae, obsecuti unum e nostro doctorum coetu Herbert
W. Schneider, Ph.D., virum et omnis philosophiae peritissimum et ad hoc munus praecipue idoneum, legatum

constituimus qui hoc nostrae benevolentiae testimonium deferret atque nostrum omnium nomine annos vobis prosperos quam plurimos exoptaret. Valete.

Dabamus Novi Eboraci Nonis Octobribus Anno Salutis MDCCCCXXXV.

XXI

Vos, viri Academici, custodes hereditatis eximiae ingeniis hominum cognitionis omnium rerum cupiditate incensorum cumulatae, quam libenter, quam speranter salutamus! Nobis enim de ista tam felici, tam late laetifica veri inquisitione saepe numero cogitantibus in memoriam redeunt eruditissimi illi qui, dum apud vestram Aulam, non pro se quisque sed pro causa ipsius scientiae, operam navabant ut fines disciplinarum multiplicum extenderent, ita de patria suisque civibus bene merebantur ut idem de ea ampliore re publica totius orbis terrarum bene meriti sint in qua omnes aequi bonique fautores in civium numerum adscribuntur. Illi sane humani nihil a se alienum putabant, neque ver, nesciebant quanto acumine Tullius in libris de officiis inscriptis adfirmaret qui civium rationem dicerent habendam, externorum negarent, eos dirimere communem humani generis societatem. Praeclare apud Vergilium Dido, regina magnanima:

Tros Tyriusque mihi nullo discrimine agetur.

Regalis sane sententia et digna quam pro sua vindicet generosissimus quisque.

Vestrates igitur nos ut olim colebamus, sic nunc laude

idcirco efferimus quod plurima in communem fructum contulerunt. Quisnam oblivisci potest quantum in arte chemica amplificanda profecerit Bunsen, in physicis Kirchhoff, in physiologia Helmholtz? Quid quod in litteris illustrandis Gervinus, in historia Schlosser et Häusser, in iure gentium Bluntschli, in theologia Rothe, in philosophia Zeller et Fischer inter omnes eminuerunt? Illis tantis ingeniis semper apertus (ut est in vestro sigillo inscriptum) constabat liber naturae et hominum, neque ullum finem investigandi patiebantur.

Nos igitur, reputantes rebus humanis hodie ingruere mutationem quae quid velit, quo evadat, nemo adhuc plane definire potest, facere non possumus quin magnam spem concipiamus vobis pro vestro antiquo more non defuturum illud insatiabile veritatis studium quo instincti per annos iam quingentos quinquaginta non modo vestrum ipsorum populum sed etiam omnes quacumque gente, quacumque stirpe oriundos a sole exoriente supra Palestinae colles usque ad occidentem in aequora Pacifici, vestri pie memores merendo reddidistis. Neque enim fieri potest ut in veritate ipsa sive indaganda sive adhibenda plus iure polleat unius mens voluntasque quam eorum dissentientium qui et natura sagaces et usu peritissimi ad rem explicandam pariter valeant. Hanc libertatem cum subtiliter disserendi tum confidenter diiudicandi haudquaquam adimere possis quin summo opere periclitetur omnis veri inquisitio. Vestra ergo praeclara historia utinam, ut voce quadam Horatiana utamur,

> servetur ad imum
> qualis ab incepto processerit et sibi constet.

Haec spes atque hoc augurium aetatis nascentis ut rite ad vos perferretur, unum e nostra doctorum societate,

Arthur F. J. Remy, Ph.D., virum praecipue idoneum a quo nihil neque rationis neque usus Germanici alienum sit, legatum constituimus. Valete.

Dabamus Novi Eboraci Kalendis Iuniis Anno Salutis MDCCCCXXXVI